SCIENTOLOGY®
THE FUNDAMENTALS OF THOUGHT

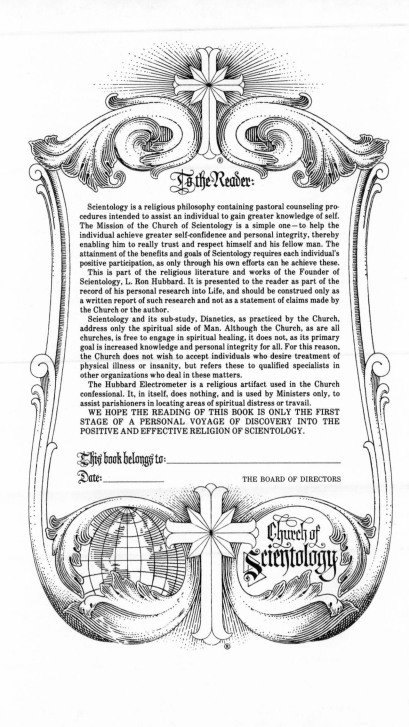

To the Reader:

Scientology is a religious philosophy containing pastoral counseling procedures intended to assist an individual to gain greater knowledge of self. The Mission of the Church of Scientology is a simple one—to help the individual achieve greater self-confidence and personal integrity, thereby enabling him to really trust and respect himself and his fellow man. The attainment of the benefits and goals of Scientology requires each individual's positive participation, as only through his own efforts can he achieve these.

This is part of the religious literature and works of the Founder of Scientology, L. Ron Hubbard. It is presented to the reader as part of the record of his personal research into Life, and should be construed only as a written report of such research and not as a statement of claims made by the Church or the author.

Scientology and its sub-study, Dianetics, as practiced by the Church, address only the spiritual side of Man. Although the Church, as are all churches, is free to engage in spiritual healing, it does not, as its primary goal is increased knowledge and personal integrity for all. For this reason, the Church does not wish to accept individuals who desire treatment of physical illness or insanity, but refers these to qualified specialists in other organizations who deal in these matters.

The Hubbard Electrometer is a religious artifact used in the Church confessional. It, in itself, does nothing, and is used by Ministers only, to assist parishioners in locating areas of spiritual distress or travail.

WE HOPE THE READING OF THIS BOOK IS ONLY THE FIRST STAGE OF A PERSONAL VOYAGE OF DISCOVERY INTO THE POSITIVE AND EFFECTIVE RELIGION OF SCIENTOLOGY.

This book belongs to:_____

Date:_____

THE BOARD OF DIRECTORS

Church of Scientology

SCIENTOLOGY:
THE FUNDAMENTALS OF THOUGHT

by

L. Ron Hubbard

PUBLICATIONS ORGANIZATION
UNITED STATES

Published by
The Church of Scientology of California
Publications Organization
United States
2723 West Temple Street
Los Angeles, California 90026

The Church of Scientology of California is a non-profit organization.
Scientology is an applied religious philosophy.
Dianetics ® and Scientology ® are registered names.

1st Printing 1956	9th Printing 1971
2nd Printing 1957	10th Printing 1972
3rd Printing 1961	11th Printing 1972
4th Printing 1963	12th Printing 1973
5th Printing 1965	13th Printing 1974
6th Printing 1967	14th Printing 1975
Pocket book edition published 1967	15th Printing July 1975
8th Printing 1968	16th Printing December 1975

17TH PRINTING SEPTEMBER 1976

Scientology

Dianetics is the trademark of L. Ron Hubbard
in respect of his published works.

ISBN 0-88404-018-6

Printed in the United States of America

CONTENTS

Important Note

In studying Dianetics and Scientology be very, very certain you never go past a word you do not fully understand.

The only reason a person gives up a study or becomes confused or unable to learn is that he or she has gone past a word or phrase that was not understood.

Trying to read past a misunderstood word results in mental "fogginess" and difficulty in comprehending the passages which follow. If you find yourself experiencing this, return to the last portion you understood easily, locate the misunderstood word and get it defined correctly—and then go on.

DIANETICS®: From the Greek dia (through) and noos *(soul), thus "through the soul"; a system for the analysis, control and development of human thought which also provides techniques for increased ability, rationality, and freedom from the discovered single source of aberrations and psychosomatic ills. Introduced May, 1950, with publication of* Dianetics: The Modern Science of Mental Health *by L. Ron Hubbard.*

SCIENTOLOGY® is an applied religious philosophy and technology resolving problems of the spirit, life and thought; discovered, developed and organized by L. Ron Hubbard as a result of his earlier Dianetic discoveries. Coming from the Latin, scio *(knowing) and the Greek* logos *(study), Scientology means "knowing how to know" or "the study of wisdom."*

INTRODUCTION

While *Scientology: The Fundamentals of Thought* was originally published as a resume of Scientology for use in translations into non-English tongues, the book itself is of inestimable value to the beginner or advanced student of the mind and life.

Containing much material new to Scientologists, the book forms a compact but broad survey of the subject.

Equipped with this book alone the student of the mind could begin a practice and perform seeming miracles in changing the states of health, ability and intelligence of people.

No such knowledge has ever before existed and no such results have ever before been attainable by Man as those which can be reached by a study of this brief volume.

Give this book to a man or a woman in trouble, a man or woman with an inquiring nature, a man or woman with associates who need a better life, and let that man or woman study this volume carefully and apply it. Change and a better life will result.

This book is a summation, if brief, of the results of 50,000 years of thinking men. Their materials, researched and capped by a quarter of a century of original search by

L. Ron Hubbard, have brought the humanities, so long outdistanced by the "exact sciences", into a state of equality, if not superiority, to physics, chemistry and mathematics.

What has been attempted by a thousand universities and foundations at a cost of billions has been completed quietly here.

This *is* how life works. This *is* how you change men and women and children for the better.

The use or neglect of this material may well determine the use or neglect of the atomic bomb by Man. Scientology is already winning in this field. In the same period in history, two of the most sweeping forces Man has known have come to fruition: a knowledge of himself and others with Scientology, and a means of destroying himself and all others by atomic fission. Which force wins depends in a large measure on your use of Scientology.

Scientology is today around the world, represented on every continent on Earth. As you read this, this very book is being translated into many non-English tongues and is being distributed to nations whose thronging multi-millions have never before been touched by Anglo-American thought.

As L. Ron Hubbard has said in an essay:

"Scientology and Scientologists are not revolutionaries. They are evolutionaries. They do not stand for overthrow. They stand for the improvement of what we have.

"Scientology is not political. When the fires of ideology threaten to consume us all, it is time to forget politics and seek reason.

"The mission of Scientology is not conquest—it is civilization. It is a war upon stupidity, the stupidity which leads us toward the Last War of All.

"To a Scientologist, the real barbarism of Earth is *stupidity*. Only in the black muck of ignorance can the irrational conflicts of ideologies germinate.

"Government, to a Scientologist, is a thing of reason, and all problems of government can be resolved by reason.

"Perhaps in yesterday one could afford the exploitation of ignorance for the sake of fancied gain. Perhaps in yesterday the study of the mind and reason was something for a summer afternoon. Perhaps in that same yesterday one amongst us could afford his irresponsibility and hate.

"But that was yesterday. Today, exploited ignorance, a dilettante attitude toward existing knowledge, and a refusal to assume one's role as a responsible member of the human race may be punished in the searing thunderclap of H-bombs released by men whose intelligence and statecraft were incapable of a better solution. Ignorant people elect ignorant rulers. And only ignorant rulers lead to war—and this time will lead to a war which will bring silence forever after to Earth.

"As your associates, their homes, their children, their possessions and all their future lie ending in a radioactive street, there won't be time for us to wish we'd worked harder, been less easily dissuaded from pressing our arguments. The copies of this book you did *not* distribute will lie there too.

"Some say they have no fear of death until the midnight of their dying is at hand. They say different then.

"Those who strike at this work out of some black well of ideological mis-orientation, some anti-social cravenness, strike at the heart of Man—for Man has been a long time on the track to reason, and Scientology can take him there.

"There is not much Earth time. We must work.

"The criminal is ignorant and stupid. Ignorance and stupidity may therefore be called criminal.

"Cause Man to lay aside his hates and listen. Freedom from ignorance is at hand. Perhaps *that* was the Kingdom of Heaven.

"There is not much Earth time in which to distribute this knowledge. This is *the* solution to our barbarism out of which we would lose all. Scientology works. *We* must work, all of us—not to harangue Man towards impossible freedoms, but to make Man civilized enough to be worthy of his freedom.

"It is time Man grew up. That is what we have in mind. For there can be but weeping in the night where ignorance, factionalism, hatred and exploitation are served by the most ferocious and final weapon of all—the H-bomb.

"Change no man's religion, change no man's politics, interrupt the sovereignty of no nation. Instead, teach Man to use what he has and what he knows to the factual creation, within *any* political reference, of a civilization on Earth for the first time.

"And so we work."

We trust you will find this volume of use in your home life and your business. We hope that by placing it in your hands, you and many others can lead better lives.

THE EDITOR

Note—This text has been organized so that a complete translation of all of it will deliver without interruption or destructive change the basics of Scientology into non-English tongues.

CHAPTER ONE

THE VITAL STATISTICS OF SCIENTOLOGY

What is Scientology?

Scientology is that branch of psychology which treats of (embraces) human ability. It is an extension of DIANETICS which is in itself an extension of old-time faculty-psychology of 400 years ago. More acceptable and normal psychology such as that begun by St. Thomas Aquinas and extended by many later authors was, in 1879, interrupted severely by one Professor Wundt, a Marxist at Leipzig University in Germany. This man conceived that man was an animal without soul and based all of his work on the principle that there was no "psyche" (a Greek word meaning "spirit").

Psychology, the study of the spirit (or mind) then came into the peculiar position of being "a study of the spirit which denied the spirit". For the subsequent decades, Wundtian "psychology" was taught broadly throughout the world. It taught that man was an animal. It taught that man could not be bettered. It taught that intelligence never changed. This subject, Wundtian psychology, became standard, mainly because of the indifference or lack of knowledge of people in charge of universities.

Scientology is actually a new but very basic psychology in the most exact meaning of the word. It can and does change behavior and intelligence, and it can and does assist people to study life.. Unlike Wundtian pseudo-psychology, it has no political aspiration. Scientology is not teaching dialectical materialism under the heading of "psychology".

The term SCIENTOLOGY is taken from the Latin word SCIO (knowing in the fullest meaning of the word) and the Greek word LOGOS (study).

Scientology, used by the trained and untrained person, improves the health, intelligence, ability, behavior, skill and appearance of people.

It is a precise and exact science, designed for an age of exact sciences.

It is employed by an AUDITOR (a Scientology practitioner) upon individuals or small or large groups of people in their presence. The Auditor makes these people, at their choice, do various exercises, and these exercises (processes) bring about changes for the better in intelligence, behavior and general competence. It is employed as well by persons in business and government to solve problems and to establish better organization.

It is also employed by the average person to bring better order into life.

How is Scientology Used?

Scientology is employed by an Auditor (one who listens and commands) as a set of drills (exercises, processes) upon the individual, and small or large groups. It is also employed as an educational (teaching) subject. It has been found that persons can be processed (drilled) in Scientology with Scientology exercises and can be freed from their major anxieties and can become brighter, more alert and more competent. BUT if they are *only* processed they have a tendency to be overwhelmed or startled, and although they may be brighter and more competent they are still held down by an ignorance of life. Therefore it is far better to teach AND process (audit, drill) a person than only to process him. In other words, the best use of Scientology is through processing and education in Scientology. In this way there is no imbalance. It is interesting that people only need to study Scientology to have some small rise in their own intelligence, behavior and competence. The study itself is therapeutic (good medicine) by actual testing.

It is also used by business and government leaders to establish or improve organization.

It is used as well by the individual at home or at his work to make a better life.

Is Scientology Valid?

Tens of thousands of case histories (reports on persons who have been processed, individual records) all sworn to (attested before public officials), are in the possession of the organizations of Scientology. No other subject on earth except physics and chemistry has had such gruelling testing (proofs, exact findings). Scientology in the hands of an expert (Auditor) can restore man's ability to handle any and all of his problems. Scientology is used by some of the largest companies (business organizations) on Earth. It is valid. It has been tested. It is the only thoroughly tested system of improving human relations, intelligence and character, and is the only one which does.

Where is there more information about Scientology?

The world headquarters for Scientology is the Hubbard College of Scientology, Saint Hill Manor, East Grinstead, Sussex, England. In addition, there are major Scientology organizations on practically every continent on earth. Scientology practitioners are validated (certified, given diplomas) by these organizations. Diplomas are given only after very exact training. A person who is skilled in Scientology procedures has a diploma from one of these organizations. A list of these organizations is provided at the back of this book.

These offices and these people can give you more information about Scientology.

There have also been many books published in English on the subject of Dianetics and Scientology. The company that is publishing the book you are reading may have more books in your language.

Can a Person without much Study use Scientology?

Scientology is practiced in daily life by enormous numbers of people who have no formal training in the humanities beyond a study of textbooks. Scientology was developed to be used by such people as well as by the trained practitioner. A person studying by himself from textbooks can use Scientology to help his fellow human beings.

What Special Use Does Scientology Have?

Scientology does things for people where nothing has been done before. It restores people's ability to handle conditions which were once considered hopeless. It increases their intelligence. It changes their competence and betters their behavior. In addition to these it brings them a better understanding of life.

————————————

Who Invented Scientology?

Scientology was discovered (found), not invented (created). It was organized by L. Ron Hubbard, an American, who has many degrees and is very skilled by reason of study. Hubbard was trained in nuclear physics at George Washington University in Washington, D. C., before he started his studies about the mind. This explains the mathematical precision of Scientology. L. Ron Hubbard has been given many honors for his work in the field of the mind. He has been assisted by one of the largest organizations, numerically speaking, in the field of the mind on Earth today, the organizations of Dianetics and Scientology. Scientology organizations contain more members than all other mental health organizations combined.

EDITOR'S NOTE

CHAPTER TWO

BASIC PRINCIPLES

Like engineering, Scientology has certain basic principles. These are necessary to a full understanding of the subject. It is not enough to know how to process (drill) people in Scientology. To be effective (good) one must also know the basic principles. Scientology is very exact. The humanities (human studies) of the past were full of opinions. Scientology is full of facts that work.

To study Scientology one should scan (skim) quickly through the basics and find something with which one can agree. Having found ONE THING (one fact) with which he can agree, one should then skim through again and find another fact. One should continue to do this until he feels some friendliness to the subject. When one has achieved this, and *only* when one has achieved this, he should then study all the basic principles. There is no effort here to be authoritarian (opinionated). No one will try to make the subject difficult.

You may have been taught that the mind (thought, the brain) is a very difficult thing to know about. This is the first principle of Scientology: It is possible to know about the mind, the spirit and Life.

The Cycle of Action

The most fundamental idea in Scientology is called

the CYCLE OF ACTION. CYCLE = a span of time with a beginning and an end = a section of the totality of time with a beginning and an end = in beginningless and endless time one can set out periods which do have a beginning and an end insofar as action is concerned. ACTION = motion or movement = an act = a consideration that motion has occurred.

In very ancient books it is written that from chaos came birth, from birth there was growth, when growth was achieved there was then a gradual decay, the decay then ended in death. After death there was chaos.

Scientology expresses this more briefly. THE CYCLE OF ACTION IS AN APPARENCY AS FOLLOWS: CREATE, then SURVIVE, then DESTROY; or Creation, Survival, Destruction. First there is Creation. Then this is followed by Survival. Then this is followed by Destruction.

APPARENCY = appears to be, as distinct from what actually IS.

This cycle is only an APPARENCY. It is what we see, what we behold, what we believe. We CONSIDER (think, believe, suppose, postulate) that it is so and then we see it so.

A child is born, he grows, he reaches manhood, he grows old, he dies. In Scientology it can be seen that none of these steps are necessary. One considers them so, and so they are "true". A man can grow old quickly or slowly. He grows old to the degree that he believes he is growing old. Because everyone AGREES that this is the way things are, they go that way. The cycle is not TRUE. It is only APPARENT. It is APPARENT because we believe we see it. It is APPARENT because we AGREE that it should be so.

The test of this principle is as follows: By using the CYCLE OF ACTION can we make anyone well or more intelligent? Thousands of tests have proven that the use of and belief in the CYCLE OF ACTION has made none well or intelligent. Therefore, no matter if we see it, there must be something wrong with it. The woman, growing old, wishing to appear younger, is protesting this CYCLE OF ACTION. She feels there is something wrong with it. There is. We have to find out what the ACTUAL cycle is before we can make people better.

ACTUAL = what is really true = that which exists despite all apparencies = that which underlies the way things seem to be = the way things really are.

THE ACTUAL CYCLE OF ACTION is as follows: CREATE, create-create-create, create-counter-create, no creation, nothingness.

CREATE = make, manufacture, construct, postulate, bring into beingness = CREATE.

Create-create-create = create again continuously one moment after the next = SURVIVAL.

Create-counter-create = to create something against a creation = to create one thing and then create something else against it = DESTROY.

No creation = an absence of any creation = no creative activity.

AN ACTUAL cycle of action then consists of various activities, but each and every one of them is creative. The cycle of action contains an APPARENCY of SURVIVAL, but this is actually only a continuous creation. The APPARENT cycle of action contains DESTRUCTION, but the ACTUAL cycle of action tells us what destruction is. DESTRUCTION is one of TWO activities. DESTRUCTION is (in terms of action) a creation of something against a creation of something else. For example, a wall is seen standing. To be apparent it is necessary that the wall be constantly created. The act of "destruction" is to exert against the wall another creativeness, that of the action or activity of knocking the wall down. Both the wall standing there and the action of knocking it down are "creative" actions. Because we may object to (argue against, dislike) a wall being knocked down, we vilify (swear at, scorn) the creativeness involved in knocking it down with the word "destructive". ACTUALITY tells us that there is no such thing as destruction. There is only creation against a creation. There is another "type of destruction" and this is NO MORE CREATION. By no longer being a party to (a member of) the wall's creation, the wall, in theory, can cease to exist for one. This is true in ACTUAL PRACTICE in Scientology.

REALITY is the way things appear. REALITY IS APPARENCY. To do anything about reality, one must search into and discover what underlies the APPARENCY. Of what does REALITY consist (what is Reality composed of)? We SEE an APPARENCY which has the CYCLE OF ACTION OF CREATE-SURVIVE-DESTROY. More basically (fundamentally) this CYCLE OF ACTION contains nothing but CREATION.

If one stops making something completely and ceases to be a party to its manufacture, it no longer exists for one. If one ceases to create, there is nothingness. When one creates something or beholds something which is created, that thing is still being created. Even if one is creating something with his left hand and has forgotten about it with his right hand, the thing still exists. In other words, one can create something without knowing it is still being created. Then one seeks to DESTROY it by a counter-creation (a creation against it). The result is a chaos created by two opposing creations.

LET US BE PRACTICAL. A science is not a science unless it is practical. A theory is no good unless it works. All the fancy and beautiful theory in the world is useless unless it has a use or a workability. Is this CYCLE OF ACTION THEORY USEFUL? It is. So long as we believe that we have to destroy with force in order to destroy at all, as long as we think in terms of destruction, we have chaos.

There is CREATING AND KNOWING ONE IS CRE-ATING. There is CREATING AND NOT KNOWING ONE IS CREATING. When one drives a car or a cart he does many things (performs many acts) which he is not AWARE OF (conscious of, knows about), and these we call AUTOMATIC ACTIONS. One is doing something and is not aware that he is doing it. One starts to create something, then places this thought still active beyond his own reach and the creation continues to occur.

KNOWINGLY CREATING SOMETHING is always the first condition. One can then purposefully CONTINUE THE CREATION UNKNOWINGLY. Everything one is doing knowingly or unknowingly one is doing here and now, in the present instant, in present time. ONE KNOWINGLY STARTED ANY CREATION in some PAST moment. But the Creation is being done in the present moment.

To stop any creation it can be established that one once knew one was creating it—finding that thought and making it known again—OR ONE CAN SIMPLY CREATE NEWLY AND CONSCIOUSLY WHAT ONE IS ALREADY CREATING UNCONSCIOUSLY (unknowingly). In either case the creation stops. The WRONG WAY is to start a new creation to counter against the old creation; when one does this he gets confusion and chaos.

FOR EXAMPLE, a man has a bad leg. He is trying to "get well". He seeks then to create a good leg. He goes to doctors and wants to be healed. The treatment is difficult and usually somewhat unsuccessful in the case of a very severely crippled leg. SOMETHING is creating a bad leg. Against this he is creating a good leg. The result is confusion and a bad leg. BUT a THIRD creativeness is present. First something was creating, we hope, a good leg. Then a counter-creation (such as an accident to his leg) counter-created a bad leg. Now he is trying to counter-create again a good leg. The result is to wipe out the ORIGINAL GOOD LEG since THAT IS THE CREATION HE IS TAKING OVER AND EXPOSING WITH HIS EFFORTS TO GET WELL. He wants a good leg. The trouble with him is the counter-creation of a bad leg. The test is factual. Have him create (by a certain Scientology process) bad legs until the counter-creation of bad legs is wiped out and the ORIGINAL CREATION OF A GOOD LEG WILL REAPPEAR. This only fails when there is no original creation of a good leg, when the original creation of a good leg is gone.

FOR EXAMPLE, a man has a job. He works at it. That is to say he create-create-creates a job throughout the days, weeks and years. As long as he makes a job, the job exists. One day he DEPENDS upon (takes for granted) this job. He no longer creates it. It ceases to exist. He has no job. The APPARENCY is that he loafed (became lazy) and was discharged. The ACTUALITY is that he no longer created a job and so didn't have one.

FOR EXAMPLE, a man depends upon a woman to keep his house for him. One day he no longer has a woman. He can't keep house EVEN THOUGH BEFORE HE MARRIED THE WOMAN HE COULD KEEP HOUSE.

FOR EXAMPLE, a man is sane. He gets the idea (creates the idea) that it would be better to be insane. He starts to go insane (having created it) and then does numberless things in order to stay sane. Here he was already creating the state of sanity. He counter-created insanity. He then counter-created sanity against insanity.

CREATION IN THIS WORK may be thought to exclude God. We are here considering only those things which man or man as a spirit can make or manufacture or think. The subject of WHO or WHAT is doing the creation does not invalidate the cycle. This is a work on the subject of the mind, not a work on the subject of the Supreme Being.

LYING is the lowest order of creativity.

There are many tests for these principles in SCIEN-TOLOGY. Such tests come under the heading of PRO-CESSING.

CHAPTER THREE

THE CONDITIONS OF EXISTENCE

There are three conditions (circumstances, qualities) of existence (apparency, reality, livingness).

These three conditions comprise (make up, constitute) life.

They are BE, DO and HAVE.

THE CONDITION OF BEING is defined as the assumption (choosing) of a category of identity. It could be said to be the role in a game and an example of beingness could be one's own name. Another example would be one's profession. Another example would be one's physical characteristics. Each or all of these things could be called one's *beingness*. Beingness is assumed by oneself or given to one's self, or is attained. For example, in the playing of a game each player has his own beingness.

THE SECOND CONDITION OF EXISTENCE IS DOING. By doing we mean action, function, accomplishment, the attainment of goals, the fulfilling of purpose, or any change of position in space.

THE THIRD CONDITION IS HAVINGNESS. By havingness we mean owning, possessing, being capable of commanding, positioning, taking charge of objects, energies or spaces.

The essential definition of *having* is to be able to touch or permeate or to direct the disposition of.

The game of life demands that one assume a beingness in order to accomplish a doingness in the direction of havingness.

These three conditions are given in an order of seniority (importance) where life is concerned. The ability to be is more important than the ability to do. The ability to do is more important than the ability to have. In most people all three conditions are sufficiently confused (chaotic, baffling) that they are best understood in reverse order. When one has clarified (brought order into) the idea of possession or havingness, one can then proceed to clarify doingness for general activity, and when this is done one understands beingness or identity.

It is an essential to a successful existence that each of these three conditions be clarified and understood. The ability to assume or to grant (give, allow) beingness is probably the highest of human virtues. It is even more important to be able to permit (allow) other people to have beingness than to be able oneself to assume it.

Beingness = Identity

If you ask an Auditor how these work in processing, he will tell you that there is a specialized form of each of these conditions. The Auditing form of Beingness is Identity. To achieve a betterment of beingness and the granting of beingness, the Auditor remedies with processing the scarcity of identities of the preclear. The preclear is often found in valences (other identities): his father's or mother's or marital partner's or any or all of thousands of possible people. He is unable to achieve or obtain (he thinks) enough identity or an identity of his own. He decries or criticizes the identities of others (fails to grant beingness to them).

He himself cannot obtain enough identity to feel he has an identity. Identity is so scarce that it's too valuable. Nobody must have one. To be with such a person is therefore an uncomfortable experience since he does not credit our identity—does not grant us beingness.

The "cure" for this is elementary. Let us say he is obviously in father's valence (identity). He got into father's valence when he found he could get no attention from mother. Observing that father got some of her attention, he took father's identity. However, let us say he didn't like father. The Auditor finds him hating "himself". "Himself" is really father.

A clever Auditor (see section under Processing) would see that while he was in father's valence, it was really mother's attention that was sought.

The Auditor does not inform his preclear of such a finding. He asks the preclear to lie about (lowest form of creativity) identities which would attract mother's attention. Then, when the preclear can do this, the Auditor would have him invent identities which would attract mother's attention.

Suddenly the preclear would be no longer in father's

valence. However, he would have been not only in father's but also in mother's valence so the same process would have to be done on father. "Lie about," the Auditor would say, "identities which would attract father's attention," then "invent one," until the preclear had many and would no longer be in mother's valence.

Solving father and mother valences is fundamental, since most people are somewhat "in them" or revolted from them. But people can be "stuck" in all sorts of identities, even bedposts when humans are too valuable to be used.

The rule is that the more a person is "stuck" in a valence or identity, the fewer he conceives to exist. And the harder he thinks it is to get attention. Thus he can become exhibitionistic (displaying himself too thoroughly, being too much *there* at all times) or he can become dispersed (hiding himself, being vague, *not there* most of the time).

People err, in identity, in being too apparent or too little apparent. The remedy of either is the remedy of their scarcity of identity.

Identity and Attention

One "needs" an identity to play the game, as covered later, but mainly to "get attention".

A being looks at things. To balance the flow of his attention, he feels he must also be looked at. Thus he becomes attention-hungry.

Unlike yellow and brown people, the white does not

usually believe he can get attention from matter or objects. The yellow and brown believe for the most part (and it is all a matter of consideration) that rocks, trees, walls, etc., can give them attention. The white man seldom believes this and so is likely to become anxious about people. Thus the white saves people, prevents famine, flood, disease and revolution for *people* as the *only* purveyors of attention are scarce. The white goes further. He often believes he can get attention only from whites and that yellow and brown peoples' attention is worthless. Thus the yellow and brown races are not very progressive, but, by and large, saner. And the white race is progressive but more frantic. The yellow and brown races do not understand white concern for "bad conditions" since what are a few million dead men? There are *plenty* of identities and there is plenty of attention, they think. The white can't understand them. Nor can they understand the white.

Attention and Identity form a group of two. Attention makes space. Identity closes space.

Attention is a method of knowing. Inattention is a method of not-knowing.

Identity is a method of making known. Lack of identity is a method of making unknown.

Valences

The whole study of valences is a fascinating one. A valence is defined as "a false identity assumed unwittingly". An identity is modified by valences. People who can be nobody may try to be everybody. People who are seeking a way out of scarcity of identity may become fixed in false valences. Nations can become fixed in valences of countries they have conquered in war, etc., etc.

A rule is that a person assumes the identity of that which gets attention. Another rule is that the person assumes the identity of that which makes him fail (for he gave it *his* attention, didn't he?)

There *is* a basic personality, a person's *own* identity. He colors or drowns this with valences as he loses or wins in life. He can be dug up.

Do = Effect

Doing can be defined as the action of creating an effect. An effect in creation is action.

An Auditor, processing a preclear, would always use "effect processes" to increase doingness.

"What effect could you create on father?" would be a typical Auditor question.

If a preclear is fixated by books, a machine, a tool or a person, the Auditor asks him to lie about, then invent effects he could create upon it. At first the preclear may be able to think of none. Then as the process is continued he may become wildly imaginative or even cruel. Further running will bring the preclear into a more comfortable frame of mind. Criminals or maniacs are people who are frantically attempting to create an effect long after they know they cannot. They cannot then create decent effects, only violent effects. Neither can they work (do).

Despair of creating an effect brings about aberration and irrational conduct. It also brings about laziness and carelessness.

Command of attention is necessary to creating an effect. Therefore when one conceives he cannot easily get attention, he seeks to create stronger effects. He creates effects to get attention. He gets attention to create effects.

As in Axiom 10 (given later), the creation of an effect is the highest purpose in this universe. Thus when one cannot create effects, he has no purpose. And thus it works out in Life. It may be all right to be a stern and unrelenting superior or parent, but such create laziness and criminals. If one cannot have an effect created upon one· (and one is known to another), very definitely harmful results will ensue.

As one believes he creates the *least* effect upon unconscious or dead people, these, as in hospitals or China, become the subject of much aberrated activity. "What effect could you create on an unconscious person (or a dead person)?" asked over and over by an Auditor obtains some astonishing results.

An artist stops his work when he believes he can no longer create an effect.

A person actually dies for lack of being able to create an effect.

BUT security often depends on being able to create *no* effect.

The whole subject of survival is bound up in no-effect. Obviously those things on which no-effect can be made, survive.

If one is anxious about survival (a foolish thing, for he can't do anything else) he becomes anxious to have about him things which resist all effects. But as his only anxiety is about the survival of a *valence* or identity, remedy of the scarcity of these can resolve the matter.

Another cycle of action, containing also the classes of effects, is START-CHANGE-and-STOP. This is the definition of control.

Havingness

As there must be a playing field (see Chapter Twelve) for a game to be held, so there must be havingness. One must be able to possess.

There are millions of methods of possession in life. The obvious one becomes overlooked. If one can see a thing he can have it—if he thinks he can.

The degree to which one can live is the degree to which one can own. To own is not to label or cart away. To own is to be able to see or touch or occupy.

One loses to the degree he is forbidden to have.

But to play a game one must be able to believe he can't have.

Effect and Have

Effect and Have form a pair like Attention and Identity.

An effect should be on or against something. Thus havingness. If one's attention never meets anything he doesn't always like it. Thus he wants objects.

Effect makes distance. Have shortens distance.

Problems

Man or any life form in this universe seems to love problems. A problem is more important than freedom. Problems keep up interest.

When a man *has* a problem very thoroughly and can't solve it, he really has too few problems. He needs more.

The insanity among the idle is a matter of problem scarcity.

A problem is defined as two or more purposes in opposition. Or Intention versus Intention.

Out of the conditions of existence above can come many complex problems.

If a man had *all* the attention in the world he would be unhappy. If he had all the identities possible, he would still be unhappy. If he could blow up Earth or create any other huge effect he wanted without limit, he would be miserable (or as insane). If he could own *everything* everywhere he would be dulled to apathy. Or so it seems. For these conditions of existence are all subordinate to the need of problems, by current Scientology reasoning and results.

Thus to have a person lie about problems or invent problems of the same size as the ones he has, or the valences he is in, or to invent data of the same or different size as the one he is fixed upon is to make a well man.

Probably the problem is the antidote to unconsciousness. It is certainly the antidote for boredom.

But in making up the problems of life he consults the conditions of existence: Be, Do, Have and their necessary partner in every case, Attention.

CHAPTER FOUR

THE EIGHT DYNAMICS

As one looks out across the confusion which is life or existence to most people, one can discover eight main divisions, to each of which apply the conditions of existence. Each division contains a cycle of action.

There could be said to be eight urges (drives, impulses) in life. These we call DYNAMICS. These are motives or motivations. We call them THE EIGHT DYNAMICS.

There is no thought or statement here that any one of these eight dynamics is more important than the others. While they are categories (divisions) of the broad game of life they are not necessarily equal to each other. It will be found amongst individuals that each person stresses one of the dynamics more than the others, or may stress a combination of dynamics as more important than other combinations.

The purpose in setting forth this division is to increase an understanding of life by placing it in compartments. Having subdivided existence in this fashion, each compartment can be inspected as itself and by itself in its relationship to the other compartments of life. In working a puzzle it is necessary to first take pieces of similar color or character and place them in groups. In studying a subject it is necessary to proceed in an orderly fashion. To promote this orderliness it is necessary to assume for our purposes these eight arbitrary compartments of life.

THE FIRST DYNAMIC—is the urge toward existence as one's self. Here we have individuality expressed fully. This can be called the SELF DYNAMIC.

THE SECOND DYNAMIC—is the urge toward existence as a sexual or bisexual activity. This dynamic actually has two divisions. Second Dynamic *(a)* is the sexual act itself and the Second Dynamic *(b)* is the family unit, including the rearing of children. This can be called the SEX DYNAMIC.

THE THIRD DYNAMIC—is the urge toward existence in groups of individuals. Any group or part of an entire class could be considered to be a part of the Third Dynamic. The school, the society, the town, the nation are each part of the Third Dynamic, and each one is a Third Dynamic. This can be called the GROUP DYNAMIC.

THE FOURTH DYNAMIC—is the urge toward existence as mankind. Whereas the white race would be considered a Third Dynamic, all the races would be considered the Fourth Dynamic. This can be called the MANKIND DYNAMIC.

THE FIFTH DYNAMIC—is the urge toward existence of the animal kingdom. This includes all living things whether vegetable or animal. The fish in the sea, the beasts of the field, or of the forest, grass, trees, flowers or anything directly and intimately motivated by life. This can be called the ANIMAL DYNAMIC.

THE SIXTH DYNAMIC—is the urge toward existence as the physical universe. The physical universe is composed of matter, energy, space and time. In Scientology we take the first letter of each of these words and coin a word, MEST. This can be called the UNIVERSE DYNAMIC.

THE SEVENTH DYNAMIC—is the urge toward existence as or of spirits. Anything spiritual, with or without identity, would come under the heading of the Seventh Dynamic. This can be called the SPIRITUAL DYNAMIC.

THE EIGHTH DYNAMIC—is the urge toward existence as Infinity. This is also identified as the Supreme Being. It is carefully observed here that the *science* of Scientology does not intrude into the Dynamic of the Supreme Being. This is called the Eighth Dynamic because the symbol of infinity stood upright makes the numeral "8". This can be called the INFINITY or GOD DYNAMIC.

Scientologists usually call these by number.

The earlier science Dianetics included Dynamics One to Four. Scientology embraces Dynamics One through Seven as known territory, scientifically demonstrated and classified.

The difficulty of stating the exact definitions of the dynamics is entirely verbal. Originally the dynamics read "the urge toward survival as—". As the science developed it became apparent that survival was only an apparency and only one facet of existence. Both the cycle of action and the three conditions of existence belong in each dynamic.

A further manifestation of these dynamics is that they could best be represented as a series of concentric circles wherein the First Dynamic would be the center and each new Dynamic would be successively a circle outside it. The idea of space adjoining enters into these Dynamics.

The basic characteristic of the individual includes his ability to so expand into the other dynamics, but when the Seventh Dynamic is reached in its entirety one will only then discover the true First Dynamic.

As an example of use of these Dynamics one discovers that a baby at birth is not perceptive beyond the First Dynamic, but as the child grows and interests extend can be seen to embrace other dynamics. As a further example of use, a person who is incapable of operating on the Third Dynamic is incapable at once of being a part of a team and so might be said to be incapable of a social existence.

As a further comment upon the Eight Dynamics, no one of these Dynamics from One to Seven is more important than any other one of them in terms of orienting the individual. While the dynamics are not of equal importance, one to the next, the ability of an individual to assume the beingness, doingness and havingness of each dynamic is an index of his ability to live.

The Eight Dynamics are used in Scientology communication and should be perfectly learned as part of the language of Scientology. The abilities and shortcomings of individuals can be understood by viewing their participation in the various dynamics.

CHAPTER FIVE

THE A-R-C TRIANGLE

There is a triangle of considerable importance in Scientology, and understanding of it gives a much greater understanding of life and an ability to use it.

The A-R-C triangle is the keystone of living associations. This triangle is the common denominator of all of life's activities. The first corner of the triangle is called Affinity. The basic definition of affinity is the consideration of distance, whether good or bad. The most basic function of complete affinity would be the ability to occupy the same space as something else.

The word "affinity" is here used to mean love, liking or any other emotional attitude. Affinity is conceived in Scientology to be something of many facets. Affinity is a variable quality. Affinity is here used as a word with the context "degree of liking". Under affinity we have the various emotional tones ranged from the highest to the lowest, and these are, in part, serenity (the highest level), enthusiasm (as we proceed downward toward the baser affinities), conservatism, boredom, antagonism, anger, covert hostility, fear, grief, apathy. This, in Scientology, is called the Tone Scale. Below apathy, affinity proceeds into solidities such as matter. Affinity is conceived to be comprised first of thought, then of emotion which contains energy particles, and then as a solid.

The second corner of the triangle is Reality. Reality could be defined as "that which appears to be". Reality is fundamentally agreement. What we agree to be real is real.

The third corner of the triangle is Communication. In human relationships this is more important than the other two corners of the triangle in understanding the composition of human relations in this universe. Communication is the solvent for all things. It dissolves all things.

The inter-relationship of the triangle becomes apparent at once when one asks, "Have you ever tried to talk to an angry man?" Without a high degree of liking and without some basis of agreement there is no communication. Without communication and some basis of emotional response there can be no reality. Without some basis for agreement and communication there can be no affinity. Thus we call these three things a triangle. Unless we have two corners of a triangle, there cannot be a third corner. Desiring any corner of the triangle, one must include the other two.

The triangle is conceived to be very spacious at the level of serenity and completely condensed at the level of matter. Thus to represent a scale for use one would draw a large triangle with a high part of the scale and succeedingly small triangles down to a dot at the bottom of the scale.

Affinity, reality and communication are the basis of the Scientology Tone Scale, which gives a prediction of human behavior as contained in *Science of Survival*.

As has already been noted, the triangle is not an

equilateral triangle. Affinity and Reality are very much less important than Communication. It might be said that the triangle begins with Communication, which brings into existence Affinity and Reality.

The most primitive Scientology definition of Communication is "Cause-Distance-Effect". The fundamental manual of Communication is the book, *Dianetics 55!*

A-R-C *are* understanding.

If you would continue a strong and able communication with someone there must be some basis for agreement. There must be some liking for the person and then communication can exist. We can see then that simple talking and writing randomly without knowledge of this would not necessarily be communication. Communication is essentially something which is sent and which is received. The intention to send and the intention to receive must both be present in some degree before an actual communication can take place. Therefore one could have conditions which appeared to be communications which were not.

Original with Scientology, as are all these concepts, the A-R-C triangle understood is an extremely useful tool or weapon in human relationships. For instance, among the A-R-C triangle laws, a communication to be received must approximate the affinity level of the person to whom it is directed.

As people descend the tone scale they become more and more difficult to communicate with, and things with which they will agree become more and more solid. Thus we have friendly discourse high on the scale and war at the bottom. Where the affinity level is hate, the agreement is solid matter, and the communications . . . bullets.

CHAPTER SIX

THE REASON WHY

Life can best be understood by likening it to a game. Since we are exterior to a great number of games we can regard them with a detached eye. If we were exterior to Life instead of being involved and immersed in the living of it, it would look to us much like games look to us from our present vantage point.

Despite the amount of suffering, pain, misery, sorrow and travail which can exist in life, the reason for existence is the same reason as one has to play a game—interest, contest, activity and possession. The truth of this assertion is established by an observation of the elements of games and then applying these elements to life itself. When we do this we find nothing left wanting in the panorama of life.

By game we mean contest of person against person, or team against team. When we say games we mean such games as baseball, polo, chess or any other such pastime. It may at one time have struck you as peculiar that men would risk bodily injury in the field of play just for the sake of "amusement". So it might strike you as peculiar that people would go on living or would enter into the "game of life" at the risk of all the sorrow, travail and pain just to have something to do. Evidently there is no greater curse than total idleness. Of course there is that condition where a person continues to play a game in which he is no longer interested.

If you will but look about the room and check off items in which you are not interested, you will discover something remarkable. In a short time you will find that there is nothing in the room in which you are not interested. You are interested in everything. However, disinterest itself is one of the mechanisms of play. In order to hide something it is only necessary to make everyone disinterested in the place where the item is hidden. Disinterest is not an immediate result of interest which has worn out. Disinterest is a commodity in itself. It is palpable, it exists.

By studying the elements (factors) of games (contests) we find ourselves in possession of the elements of life.

Life is a game. A game consists of *freedom, barriers* and *purposes*. This is a scientific fact, not merely an observation.

Freedom exists amongst barriers. A totality of barriers and a totality of freedom alike are no-game conditions. Each is similarly cruel. Each is similarly purposeless.

Great revolutionary movements fail. They promise unlimited freedom. That is the road to failure. Only stupid visionaries chant of endless freedom. Only the afraid and the ignorant speak of and insist upon unlimited barriers.

When the relation between freedom and barriers becomes too unbalanced, an unhappiness results.

"Freedom from" is all right only so long as there is a place to be free *to*. An endless desire for *freedom from* is a perfect trap, a fear of all things.

Barriers are composed of inhibiting (limiting) ideas, space, energy, masses and time. Freedom in its entirety would be a total absence of these things—but it would also be a freedom without thought or action, an unhappy condition of total nothingness.

Fixed on too many barriers, man yearns to be free. But launched into total freedom he is purposeless and miserable.

There is *freedom* amongst barriers. If the barriers are known and the freedoms are known there can be life, living, happiness, a game.

The restrictions of a government, or a job, give an employee his freedom. Without known restrictions, an employee is a slave, doomed to the fears of uncertainty in all his actions.

Executives in business and government can fail in three ways and thus bring about a chaos in their department. They can:

(1) seem to give endless freedom;
(2) seem to give endless barriers;
(3) make neither freedom nor barriers certain.

Executive competence, therefore, consists of imposing and enforcing an adequate balance between their people's freedom and the unit's barriers and in being precise and consistent about those freedoms and barriers. Such an executive adding only in himself initiative and purpose can have a department with initiative and purpose.

An employee, buying and/or insisting upon freedom only, will become a slave. Knowing the above facts he must insist upon a workable balance between freedom and barriers.

An examination of the dynamics above will demonstrate the possibility of a combination of teams. Two group dynamics can engage one another as teams. The self dynamic can ally itself with the animal dynamic against, let us say, the universe dynamic and so have a game. In other words, the dynamics are an outline of possible teams and interplays. As everyone is engaged in several games, an examination of the dynamics will plot and clarify for him the various teams he is playing on and those he is playing against. If an individual can discover that he is only playing on the self dynamic and that he belongs to no other team it is certain that this individual will lose, for he has before him seven remaining dynamics. And the self dynamic is seldom capable of besting by itself all the remaining dynamics. In Scientology we call this condition the "only one". Here is selfish determinism in the guise of self-determinism and here is an individual who will most certainly be overwhelmed. To enjoy life one must be willing to be some part of life.

There is the principle in Scientology called pan-determinism. This could be loosely defined as determining the activities of two or more sides in a game simultaneously. For instance, a person playing chess is being self-determined and is playing chess against an opponent. A person who is pan-determined on the subject of chess could play both sides of the board.

A being is pan-determined about any game to which he is senior. He is self-determined only in a game to which he is junior. For instance, a general of an army is pan-determined concerning an argument between two privates or even two companies of his command. He is pan-determined in this case; but when he confronts another army, led by another general, he becomes self-determined. The game in this wise could be said to be larger than himself. The game becomes even larger than this when the general seeks to play the parts of all the political heads which should be above him. This is the main reason why dictatorship doesn't work. It is all but impossible for one man to be pan-determined about the entire system of games which comprise a nation. He starts taking sides and then to that degree becomes much less than the government which he is seeking to run.

It has been stylish in past ages to insist upon only freedom. The French Revolution furnishes an excellent example for this. In the late part of the 18th century, the nobles of France became so self-determined against the remainder of the country and were so incapable of taking the parts of the populace that the nobles were destroyed. Immediately the populace itself sought to take over the government, and, being trained and being intensely anti-pathetic to any and all restraints, their war cry became "Freedom". They had no further restrictions or barriers. The rules of government were thrown aside. Theft and brigandage took the place of economics. The populace, therefore, found itself in a deeper trap and discovered itself to be involved with a dictatorship which was far more restrictive than anything it had experienced before the Revolution.

Although man continually uses "Freedom" for his war cry he only succeeds in establishing further entrapment for himself. The reason for this is a very simple one. A game consists of freedom *and* barriers *and* purposes. When man drops the idea of restrictions or barriers he loses at once control over barriers. He becomes self-determined about barriers and not pan-determined, thus he cannot control the barriers. The barriers left uncontrolled trap him then and there.

The dwindling spiral of the apparency Create-Survive-Destroy comes about directly when man shuns barriers. If he considers all restrictions and barriers his enemies, he is of course refusing to control them in any way and thus he starts his own dwindling spiral. A race which is educated to think in terms of freedom only is very easily entrapped. No one in the nation will take responsibility for restrictions, therefore restrictions apparently become less and less. Actually they become more and more. As these restrictions lessen, so lessens the freedom of the individual. One cannot be free from a wall unless there is a wall. Lacking any restrictions life becomes purposeless, random, chaotic.

A good manager must be capable of taking responsibility for restrictions in that freedom, to exist, must have barriers. A failure to take initiative on the subject of restrictions or barriers causes them to arise all by themselves and exist without consent or direction.

There are various states of mind which bring about

happiness. That state of mind which insists only upon freedom can bring about nothing but unhappiness. It would be better to develop a thought pattern which looked for new ways to be entrapped, and things to be trapped in, than to suffer the eventual total entrapment of dwelling upon freedom only. A man who is willing to accept restrictions and barriers, and is not afraid of them, is free. A man who does nothing but fight restrictions and barriers will usually be trapped. The way to have endless war is "abandon" all war.

As it can be seen in any game, purposes become counter-posed. There is a matter of purpose-counter-purpose in almost any game played in a field with two teams. One team has the idea of reaching the goal of the other, and the other has the idea of reaching the goal of the first. Their purposes are at war, and this warring of purposes makes a game.

The war of purposes gives us what we call problems. A problem consists of two or more purposes opposed. It does not matter what problem you face or have faced, the basic anatomy of that problem is purpose-counter-purpose.

In actual testing in Scientology it has been discovered that a person begins to suffer from problems when he does not have enough of them. There is the old saw (maxim) that if you want a thing done, give it to a busy man to do. Similarly if you want a happy associate, make sure that he is a man who can have lots of problems.

SELF-DETERMINISM is a condition of determining the actions of self. It is a First (Self) Dynamic action and leaves the remaining seven undetermined or, in actuality, in opposition to the self. Thus if one wants to take on the rest of life in a free-for-all fight, one could be entirely insistent upon total self-determinism. As the remainder of the dynamics must have a say in one's self to function, they fight at once any attempt at total self-determinism.

PAN-DETERMINISM means determining the action of self and others. It means wider determinism than self. In an aberrated fashion we see this in an effort to control all others to aggrandize (make important) self. Pan-determinism is *across* determinism or determinism of two sides. If one controls (monitors) both sides of a chess game one is "above" the game.

One is self-determined, then, in any situation in which he is fighting. He is pan-determined in any situation which he is controlling.

To become pan-determined rather than only self-determined, it is necessary to view both sides.

A problem is an intention-counter-intention. It is then something that has two opposing sides. By creating problems one tends to view both sides in opposition and so becomes pan-determined.

Thus a problem only *appears* to be necessary to man. The problem is the closest reality man has to pan-determinism. In processing, the invention of problems then shows a wider view and so exteriorizes one from difficulty.

From this we get the oddity of a high incidence of

neurosis in the families of the rich. These people have very little to do and have very few problems. The basic problems of food, clothing and shelter are already solved for them. We would suppose, then, if it were true that an individual's happiness depended only upon his freedom, that these people would be happy. However, they are not happy. What brings about their unhappiness? It is the lack of problems.

Although successful processing in Scientology would depend upon taking all three elements of games into consideration—and indeed that is the secret of bettering people: taking freedom, barriers and purposes into consideration and balancing them—it is true that you could make a man well simply by sitting down with him and asking him to invent problems one after the other. The invention of synthetic problems would be found to free his mind and make him more able. Of course, there is another factor involved in this in that it is he who is inventing the problems and therefore he is becoming pan-determined about problems rather than being in one place with all problems opposed to him.

An unhappy man is one who is considering continually how to become free. One sees this in the clerk who is continually trying to avoid work. Although he has a great deal of leisure time he is not enjoying any part of it. He is trying to avoid contact with people, objects, energies and spaces. He eventually becomes trapped in a sort of lethargy. If this man could merely change his mind and start "worrying" about how he could get more work to do, his happiness level would increase markedly. One who is plotting continually how to get out of things will be miserable. One who is plotting how to get into things has a much better chance of becoming happy.

There is, of course, the matter of being forced to play games in which one has no interest—a war into which one is drafted is an excellent example of this. One is not interested in the purposes of the war and yet one finds himself fighting it. Thus there must be an additional element, and this element is "the power of choice".

One could say, then, that life is a game and that the ability to play a game consists of tolerance for freedom and barriers and an insight into purposes, with the power of choice over participation.

These four elements, freedom, barriers, purposes and power of choice, are the guiding elements of life. There are only two factors above these, and both of them are related to these. The first is the ability to create, with, of course, its negative, the ability to uncreate; and the second is the ability to make a postulate (to consider, to say a thing and have it be true). This, then, is the broad picture of life, and these elements are used in its understanding, in bringing life into focus and in making it less confusing.

CHAPTER SEVEN

THE PARTS OF MAN

The individual man is divisible (separable) into three parts (divisions).

> The first of these is the spirit, called in Scientology the *Thetan*.
> The second of these parts is the *Mind*.
> The third of these parts is the *Body*.

Probably the greatest discovery of Scientology and its most forceful contribution to the knowledge of mankind has been the isolation, description and handling of the human spirit, accomplished in July, 1951, in Phoenix, Arizona. I established along scientific rather than religious or humanitarian lines that that thing which is the person, the personality, is separable from the body and the mind at will and without causing bodily death or mental derangement.

In ages past there has been considerable controversy concerning the human spirit or soul, and various attempts to control man have been effective in view of his almost complete ignorance of his own identity. Latterly spiritualists isolated from the person what they called the astral body, and with this they were able to work for various purposes of their own. In Scientology the spirit itself was separated from what the spiritualists called the astral body and there should be no confusion between these two things. As you know that you are where you are at this moment, so you would know if you, a spirit, were detached from your mind and body. Man had not discovered this before because, lacking the technologies of Scientology, he had very little reality upon his detachment from his mind and body and therefore conceived himself to be at least in part a mind and a body. The entire cult of communism is based upon the fact that one lives only one life, that there is no hereafter and that the individual has no religious significance. Man at large has been close to this state for at least the last century. The state (condition) is of a very low order, excluding as it does all self-recognition.

The Spirit

The thetan (spirit) is described in Scientology as having no mass, no wave-length, no energy and no time or location in space except by consideration or postulate. The spirit, then, is not a *thing*. It is the *creator* of things.

The usual residence of the thetan is in the skull or near the body. A thetan can be in one of four conditions. The first would be entirely separate from a body or bodies, or even from this universe. The second would be near a body and knowingly controlling the body. The third would be in the body (the skull) and the fourth would be an inverted condition whereby he is compulsively away from the body and cannot approach it. There are degrees (subdivisions) of each one of these four states (conditions). The most optimum of these conditions, from the standpoint of man, is the second.

A thetan is subject to deterioration. This is at first

difficult to understand since the entirety of his activity consists of considering or postulating. He uses, through his postulates, various methods of controlling a body. That he does deteriorate is manifest, but that he can at any moment return to an entirety of his ability is also factual. In that he associates beingness with mass and action, he does not consider himself as having an individual identity or name unless he is connected with one or more of the games of life.

The processes of Scientology can establish this for the individual with greater or lesser rapidity, and one of the many goals of processing in Scientology is to "exteriorize" the individual and place him in the second condition above, since it has been discovered that he is happier and more capable when so situated.

The Mind

The *mind* is a communication and control system between the thetan and his environment. The mind is a network of communications and pictures, energies and masses, which are brought into being by the activities of the thetan versus the physical universe or other thetans. A thetan establishes various systems of control so that he can continue to operate a body and through the body operate things in the physical universe, as well as other bodies. The most obvious portion of the mind is recognizable by anyone not in serious condition. This is the "mental image picture". In Scientology we call this mental image picture a *facsimile* when it is a "photograph" of the physical universe sometime in the past. We call this mental image picture a *mock-up* when it is created by the thetan or for the thetan and does not consist of a photograph of the physical universe. We call a mental image picture a "hallucination", or more properly an automaticity (something uncontrolled) when it is created by another and seen by self.

Various phenomena connect themselves with this entity called the mind. Some people closing their eyes see only blackness, some people see pictures. Some people see pictures made by body reactions. Some people see only black screens. Others see golden lines. Others see spaces. But the keynote of the entirety of the system called the mind is postulate and perception. Easily ten thousand new, separate mental phenomena, not hitherto seen by earlier observers, have been classified in Scientology and Dianetics (that branch of Scientology which applies only to the mind).

The thetan receives, by the communication system called the mind, various impressions, including direct views of the physical universe. In addition to this he receives impressions from past activities and, most important, he himself, being close to a total knowingness, conceives things about the past and future which are independent of immediately present stimuli. The mind is not in its entirety a stimulus-response mechanism as old Marxist psychology, as once taught in universities, would have one believe. The mind has three main divisions. The first of these could be called the *analytical mind*, the second the *reactive mind*, and the third the *somatic mind.*

The Analytical Mind

The *analytical mind* combines perceptions of the

immediate environment, of the past (via pictures) and estimations of the future into conclusions which are based upon the realities of situations. The analytical mind combines the potential knowingness of the thetan with the conditions of his surroundings and brings him to independent conclusions. This mind could be said to consist of visual pictures either of the past or of the physical universe, monitored by, and presided over by, the knowingness of a thetan. The keynote of the analytical mind is awareness. One knows what one is concluding and knows what one is doing.

The Reactive Mind

The *reactive mind* is a stimulus-response mechanism, ruggedly built, and operable in trying circumstances. The reactive mind never stops operating. Pictures of the environment, of a very low order, are taken by this mind even in some states of unconsciousness. The reactive mind acts below the level of consciousness. It is the literal stimulus-response mind. Given a certain stimulus it gives a certain response. The entire subject of Dianetics (through mind) concerned itself mainly with this one mind.

While it is an order of thinkingness, the ability of the reactive mind to conclude rationally is so poor that we find in the reactive mind those various aberrated impulses which are gazed upon as oddities of personality, eccentricities, neuroses and psychoses. It is this mind which stores up all the bad things that have happened to one and throws them back to him again in moments of emergency or danger so as to dictate his actions along lines which have been considered "safe" before. As there is little thinkingness involved in this, the courses of action dictated by the reactive mind are often not safe, but highly dangerous.

The reactive mind is entirely literal in its interpretation of words and actions. As it takes pictures and receives impressions during moments of unconsciousness, a phrase uttered when a blow is struck is likely to be literally interpreted by the reactive mind and becomes active upon the body and analytical mind at later times. The mildest stage of this would be arduous training, wherein a pattern is laid into the mind for later use under certain given stimuli.

A harsh and less workable level is the hypnotic trance condition to which the mind is susceptible. Made impressionable by fixed attention, words can be immediately implanted into the reactive mind which become operable under restimulation at later times.

An even lower level in the reactive mind is that one associated with blows, drugs, illness, pain and other conditions of unconsciousness. Phrases spoken over an anaesthetized person can have a later effect upon that person. It is not necessarily true that each and every portion of an operation is painstakingly "photographed" by the reactive mind of the unconscious patient, but it is true that a great many of these stimuli are registered. Complete silence, in the vicinity of a person under anaesthetic or a person who is unconscious or in deep pain, is mandatory if one would preserve the mental health of that person or patient afterwards.

Probably the most therapeutic action which could occur to an individual would be, under Scientology processing, the separation of the thetan from the mind so that the thetan, under no duress and with total knowingness, could view himself and his mind and act accordingly. However, there is a type of exteriorization which is the most aberrative of all traumatic (mentally injurious) actions. This is the condition when an individual is brought, through injury or surgery or shock, very close to death so that he exteriorizes from body and mind. This exteriorization under duress is sudden, and to the patient inexplicable, and is in itself very shocking. When this has occurred to an individual, it is certain that he will suffer mentally from the experience afterwards.

It could be said that when the reactive mind contains these sudden shocks of exteriorization under duress, attempts to exteriorize the individual later by Scientology are more difficult. However, modern processing has overcome this. The phenomenon of exteriorization under duress is accompanied at times by energy explosions in the various facsimiles of the mind, and these cross-associate in the reactive mind. Therefore, people become afraid of exteriorization, and at times people are made ill simply by discussing the phenomenon, due to the fact that they have exteriorized under duress, during some operation, or during some accident.

Exteriorization under duress is the characteristic of death itself. Therefore, exteriorization or the departure of the soul is generally associated with death in the minds of most people. It is not necessarily true that one is dead because he exteriorizes, and it is definitely not true that exteriorization not accompanied by a shock, pain or duress is at all painful. Indeed, it is quite therapeutic.

The Somatic Mind

The third portion of the mind is the *somatic mind*. This is an even heavier type of mind than the reactive mind since it contains no thinkingness and contains only actingness. The impulses placed against the body by the thetan through various mental machinery arrive at the voluntary, involuntary and glandular levels. These have set methods of analysis for any given situation and so respond directly to commands given.

Unfortunately the somatic mind is subject to each of the minds higher in scale above it and to the thetan. In other words, the thetan can independently affect the somatic mind. The analytical mind can affect the somatic mind. The reactive mind can affect the somatic mind. Thus we see that the neurons, the glandular system, the muscles and masses of the body are subject to various impulses, each one of a lower order than the next. Thus it is not odd to discover what we call "psychosomatic" illness. A condition exists here where the thetan does not have an awareness of burdening the somatic mind with various commands or derangements. Neither does the thetan have an awareness of his own participation in the analytical mind causing this action against the body.

In that the thetan is seldom aware of the reactive mind, it is possible then for the reactive mind, with its stimulus-response content, to impinge itself directly, and without further recourse or advice, upon the neurons, muscles and glandular system of the body. In that the reactive mind can hold a fixed command in place, causing a derangement in the somatic mind, it is possible then for illness to exist, for bizarre pains to be felt, for actual physical twists and aberrations to occur, without any conscious knowledge on the part of the thetan. This we call physical illness caused by the mind. In brief, such illness is caused by perceptions received in the reactive mind during moments of pain and unconsciousness.

Whether the facsimile in the mind is received while the thetan is awake or unconscious, the resulting mass of the energy picture is energy just as you see energy in an electric light bulb or from the flames of a fire. At one time it was considered that mental energy was different from physical energy. In Scientology it has been discovered that mental energy is simply a finer, higher level physical energy. The test of this is conclusive in that a thetan "mocking up" (creating) mental image pictures and thrusting them into the body can increase the body mass and, by casting them away again, can decrease the body mass. This test has actually been made and an increase of as much as 30 pounds, actually measured on scales, has been added to, and subtracted from, a body by creating "mental energy". Energy is energy. It has different wave-lengths and different characteristics. The mental image pictures are capable of reacting upon the physical environment, and the physical environment is capable of reacting on mental image pictures. Thus the mind actually consists of spaces, energies and masses of the same order as the physical universe, if lighter and different in size and wave-length. For a much more comprehensive picture of the mind one should read *Dianetics: The Original Thesis* and *Dianetics: The Modern Science of Mental Health*. These were written before the discoveries of the upper levels of beingness were made and are a very complete picture of the mind itself, its structure and what can be done to it and with it.

The Body

The third part of man is the physical *body*. This can best be studied in such books as *Grey's Anatomy* and other anatomical texts. This is the province of the medical doctor and, usually, the old-time psychiatrist or psychologist who were involved in the main in body worship. The body is a purely structural study, and the actions and reactions amongst its various structures are complex and intensely interesting.

When Scientology established bio-physics, it did so because of the various discoveries which had accumulated concerning mental energy in its reaction against physical energy, and the activities which took place in the body because of these interactions. Bio-physics only became feasible when it was discovered in Scientology that a fixed electrical field existed surrounding a body entirely independent of, but influenceable by, the human mind. The body exists in its own space. That space is created by "anchor points" (points which are anchored in a space different to the physical universe space around a body). The complexity of these anchor points can cause an independent series of electronic flows which can occasion much discomfort to the individual. The balance structure of the body and even its joint action and physical characteristics can be changed by changing this electrical field which exists at a distance from, or within, the body.

The electrical field is paramount and monitors the actual

physical structure of the body. Thus the body is not only influenced by the three minds, it is influenced as well by its own electrical field. An expert Scientologist can discover for the average person this field, and can bring about its adjustment, although this is very far from the primary purpose of the Scientologist.

The use of electrical shocks upon a body for any purpose is therefore very dangerous and is not condoned by sensible men. Of course, the use of electrical shock was never intended to be therapeutic, but was intended only to bring about obedience by duress, and, as far as it can be discovered, to make the entirety of insanity a horror. Electrical shock deranges the electronic field in the vicinity of the body and is always succeeded by bad health or physical difficulties and never does otherwise than hasten the death of the person. It has been stated by people using electric shock that if they were denied euthanasia (the right to kill people who were considered to be a burden on a society) they would at least use partial euthanasia in the form of electric shock, brain surgery and drugs. These treatments in some large percentage of cases, however, effected euthanasia as they were expected to do.

A knowledge of both the mental and physical structure of the body would be necessary in order to treat the body, and this knowledge has not existed prior to Scientology. The medical doctor has achieved many results by working purely with structure and bio-chemical products, and in the field of emergency surgery and obstetrics and orthopaedics, he is indispensable in the society. Medicine, however, has not previously even contained a definition for "mind" and is not expected to ‚

invade the field which belongs properly to Scientology.

These three parts of man, the thetan, the mind and the body, are each one different studies, but they influence each other markedly and continually. Of the three, the senior entity is the thetan, for without the thetan there would be no mind or animation in the body, while without a body or a mind there is still animation and life in the thetan. The thetan *is* the person. You are *you in* a body.

Many speculations in the field of para-Scientology have been made. Para-Scientology includes all of the uncertainties and unknown territories of life which have not been completely explored and explained. However, as studies have gone forward, it has become more and more apparent that the senior activity of life is that of the thetan, and that in the absence of the spirit no further life exists. In the insect kingdom it is not established whether or not each insect is ordered by a spirit or whether one spirit orders enormous numbers of insects. It is not established how mutation and evolution occur (if they do), and the general Authorship of the physical universe is only speculated upon, since Scientology does not invade the Eighth Dynamic.

Some facts, however, are completely known. The first of these is that the individual himself is a spirit controlling a body via a mind. The second of these is that the thetan is capable of making space, energy, mass and time. The third of these is that the thetan is separable from the body without the phenomenon of death, and can handle and control a body from well outside it. The fourth of these is that the thetan does not care to remember the life which he has just lived, after he has parted from the body and the mind. The fifth of these is that a person dying always exteriorizes. The sixth of these is that the person, having exteriorized, usually returns to a planet and procures, usually, another body of the same type of race as before.

In para-Scientology there is much discussion about "between lives areas" and other phenomena which might have passed at one time or another for heaven or hell, but it is established completely that a thetan is immortal and that he himself cannot actually experience death and counter-feits it by forgetting. It is adequately manifest that a thetan lives again and that he is very anxious to put something on the "time track" (something for the future) in order to have something to come back to, thus we have the anxieties of sex. There must be additional bodies for the next life.

It is obvious that what we create in our societies during this lifetime affects us during our next lifetime. This is quite different from the "belief", or the idea, that this occurs. In Scientology we have very little to do with forcing people to make conclusions. An individual can experience these things for himself and unless he can do so no one expects him to accept them.

The manifestation that our hereafter is our next life entirely alters the general concept of spiritual destiny. There is no argument whatsoever with the tenets of faith since it is not precisely stated, uniformly, by religions that one immediately goes to a heaven or hell. It is certain that an individual experiences the effect of the civilization which he has had part in creating, in his next lifetime. In other words, the individual comes back. He has a responsibility for what goes on today since he will experience it tomorrow.

Sex has been overweighted in importance in old psychotherapy, an importance more or less disgraced at this time. Sex is only one of numerous creative impulses. An anxiety about sex, however, occurs when an individual begins to believe that there will not be a body for him to have during the next lifetime.

The common denominator of all aberration (mental derangement) is cessation of creation. As sex is only one kind of creation and a rather low order of it, it will be seen that unhappiness could stem from various cessations of creation. Death itself is a cessation of creation. One stops creating the identity John Jones and the environment and things of John Jones. He stops because he believes he cannot, himself, continue this creation without the assistance of a body, having become dependent upon a mind and a body, the first to do his thinking for him and the second to do his acting. An individual becoming sufficiently morose on the ideas of creation can actually bring about the condition of an inability to create.

Control

It will be seen that the three parts of man are intimately associated with *control*. The anatomy of control is start, change and stop. The loss of control takes place with the loss of pan-determinism. When one becomes too partisan, braces himself too solidly against the remainder of the environment, he no longer controls the environment to the degree that he might and so is unable to start, change and stop the environment.

It is a scientific definition in Scientology that control consists of start, change and stop. These three manifestations can be graphed alongside the apparent cycle of action: create, survive, destroy. Any person is somewhere along this curve. An individual who is bent mainly upon survival is intent, usually, upon changing things. An individual who is close to being destroyed is bent mainly upon stopping things. An individual who has a free heart and mind about life is bent upon creating things.

There could be three things wrong with any person, and these would be the inability to start, the inability to change, the inability to stop. Insanity, for the most part, is an inability to stop. A neurosis is a habit which, worsening, flies entirely out of control. One is stopped so often in life that he becomes an enemy of stopping and dislikes stopping so intensely that he himself will not stop things. Neurosis and psychosis of all classes are entirely inabilities to start, to change or to stop.

In the matter of the parts of man we discover that all things are initiated by the thetan so far as action, activity and behavior are concerned. After such an initiation he can be blunted or warped from course and acted upon in such a way that his attention becomes too fixed along one line or another and begins to suffer from these three inabilities. However, each one of the parts of man is subject to the anatomy of control.

An individual begins first by being unable himself, without help, to start, to change and to stop. Then the mind may become prone to these disabilities and is unable to start, change or to stop at will. Then the body itself can become subject to these three disabilities and is unable to start, to change and to stop. The oddity is, however, that an environment can so work upon a thetan that his body becomes disabled through no choice of his own. Similarly the reactive mind can become disabled through no choice of either the body or the thetan. But the thetan himself, beyond observing the effect of various causes and having initiated the thought to be there, can only become disabled by becoming too partisan, by becoming too little pan-determined, and so bringing himself into difficulties. These difficulties, however, are entirely the difficulties of consideration. As the thetan considers, so he is. In the final analysis the thetan has no problems of his own. The problems are always "other people's problems" and must exist in the mind or the body or in other people or his surroundings for him to have problems. Thus his difficulties are, in the main, difficulties of staying in the game and keeping the game going.

If a thetan can suffer from anything, it is being out-created (created against too thoroughly). The manifestations of being out-created would be the destruction of his own creations and the overpowering presence of other creations. Thus a thetan can be brought to believe that he is trapped if he is out-created.

In past dissertations on the subject of the mind and philosophies of life there was a great deal of speculation and very little actual proof. Therefore, these philosophies were creations, and one philosopher was at work out-creating another philosopher. In Scientology we have this single difference. We are dealing with discoveries. The only things created about Scientology are the actual books and works in which Scientology is presented. The phenomena of Scientology are discovered and are held in common by all men and all life forms. There is no effort in Scientology to out-create each and every thetan that comes along. It is, of course, possible to conceive Scientology as a creation, and to conceive that it is overwhelming. It should be viewed otherwise, for it is intended as an assistance to life at large, to enable life to make a better civilization and a better game. There are no tenets in Scientology which cannot be demonstrated with entirely scientific procedures.

CHAPTER EIGHT

CAUSATION OF KNOWLEDGE

Scientology as a science is composed of many axioms (self-evident truths, as in geometry). There are some fifty-eight of these axioms in addition to the two hundred more axioms of Dianetics which preceded the Scientology axioms.

The first axiom in Scientology is:

Axiom 1. Life is basically a static. (Definition: A life static has no mass, no motion, no wave-length, no location in space or in time. It has the ability to postulate and to perceive.)

Definition: In Scientology, the word "postulate" means to cause a thinkingness or consideration. It is a specially applied word and is defined as causative thinkingness.

Axiom 2. The static is capable of considerations, postulates and opinions.

Axiom 3. Space, energy, objects, form and time are the result of considerations made and/or agreed upon or not by the static, and are perceived solely because the static considers that it can perceive them.

Axiom 4. Space is a viewpoint of dimension. (Space is caused by looking out from a point. The only actuality of space is the agreed-upon consideration that one perceives through something, and this we call space.)

Axiom 5. Energy consists of postulated particles in space. (One considers that energy exists and that he can perceive energy. One also considers that energy behaves according to certain agreed-upon laws. These assumptions or considerations are the totality of energy.)

Axiom 6. Objects consist of grouped particles and solids.

Axiom 7. Time is basically a postulate that space and particles will persist. (The rate of their persistence is what we measure with clocks and the motion of heavenly bodies.)

Axiom 8. The apparency of time is the change of position of particles in space.

Axiom 9. Change is the primary manifestation of time.

Axiom 10. The highest purpose in the universe is the creation of an effect.

These first ten axioms of Scientology are the most fundamental "truths" (by which we mean commonly held considerations). Here we have thought and life and the physical universe in their relation, one to the other. Regardless of further considerations, ideas, assumptions and conditions there lies beneath them these first ten truths.

It is as though one had entered into an honorable bargain

with fellow beings to hold these things in common. Once this is done, or once such a "contract" or agreement exists, one has the fundamentals of a universe. Specialized considerations based on the above make one or another kind of universe.

The physical universe which we see around us and in which we live was created on these fundamentals without regard to Who created it. Its creation was agreed upon. In order to perceive it, one must agree that it exists.

There are three classes of universes. There is first, foremost and most evident, the physical universe of spaces, stars, suns, land, sea, air and living forms. Then there is the other fellow's universe which may or may not be agreed upon by his associates. This he holds to himself. The phenomenon of this universe is included in the field of the "mind" as described earlier. Then, listed last here, but first perceived, is one's own universe.

The phenomenon of universes is an interesting one, since one's own universe can be overwhelmed by the universes of others. These in Scientology we call valences (extra personalities, cells, apparent beingnesses). Valences and universes are the same thing, essentially.

For example, one while living in the physical universe can be overpowered by the universe of, let us say, father. While one still retains his own valence or identity, one is yet acting or thinking or suffering or feeling somewhat like father. Even though one is by oneself, there is this additional apparent beingness. Although father is absent, his commands are still present. Thus we get such things as "duty", "obedience", "training" and even "education". Each one of these is caused by some part of another universe to a greater or lesser degree.

Regardless of how one reacts to universes, he still remains in some degree himself. It is the effort of many to struggle against universes or valences. In fact, this is a game and the essence of games. The totality of the impulse of aberrated people is the effort to separate one's own self as a thetan from the various universes with which he feels himself too intimately associated. One is only oppressed by a universe when he feels he can have nothing of that universe. One is only victimized by "Father's universe" when one is in protest against father. One protests against the physical universe only when he feels that he can have no part of it or does not belong in it or, as in religion, is not looked upon kindly by what he conceives to be the Creator of the physical universe. There is a basic law about universes: the postulates of the creator of any universe are the postulates which "work" in that universe. Thus one may feel uncomfortable in the universe of another.

Universes, as considered in games earlier, could be considered the playing fields of life. One plays willingly or one plays unwillingly. When one begins to play unwillingly he is apt to discover himself victimized by and interiorized into the universe of some game. It is against this phenomenon that a person protests. Consider the matter of a jail. On the surface of it, as Voltaire discovered, a jail provides food and shelter and leisure time. This would seem to be the ambition of many people, but the jail provides as well a restriction without one's consent. The only difference between being in jail and being the king in a castle, so far as liberty is concerned, is one's own desires in the matter and one's own ability to command one's environment. As a king in a castle one would be causative. His will, statement, thinkingness would have an effect upon others. Being in jail, one is an effect in that the thinkingness of others finds him its target. Here we have in terms of universes the most rudimentary example of cause and effect.

We must, however, assume, because it is so evident, that an individual only gets into traps and circumstances he intends to get into. Certain it is that, having gotten into such a position, he may be unwilling to remain in it, but a trap is always preceded by one's own choice of entrance. We must assume a very wide freedom of choice on the part of a thetan, since it is almost impossible to conceive how a thetan could get himself trapped even though he consented to it. By actual demonstration a thetan goes through walls, barriers, vanishes space, appears anywhere at will and does other remarkable things. It must be, then, that an individual can be trapped only when he considers that he is trapped. In view of the fact that the totality of existence is based upon his own considerations, we find that the limitations he has must have been invited by himself— otherwise they could not be eradicated by the individual under processing, since the only one who is present with the preclear is the Auditor, and past associates of the preclear, while not present, do desensitize, under auditing, in the preclear's mind. Therefore it must have been the preclear who kept them there. The preclear by processing can resolve all of his difficulties without going and finding other persons or consulting other universes. Thus the totality of entrapment, aberration, even injury, torture, insanity and other distasteful items are basically considerations a thetan is making and holding right now in present time. This must be the case since time itself is a postulate or consideration on his own part.

The greatest philosophical clamor or quarrel has been waged around the subject of "knowledge", and there is nothing preposterous on the subject of knowledge that cannot be found in the philosophical texts. The superiority and ascendancy of Scientology depends upon the fact that it has transcended this philosophical quarrel on the subject of knowingness, and Scientology contains in itself the basics of knowledge.

By knowledge we mean assured belief, that which is known, information, instruction, enlightenment, learning, practical skill. By knowledge we mean data, factors and whatever can be thought about or perceived.

The reason why knowledge has been misunderstood in philosophy is that it is only half the answer. There is no allness to knowledge. By definition, knowledge is that which is perceived or learned or taken from another source. This patently then means that when one learns he is being an effect.

We see in Axiom 10 that "the highest purpose in the universe is the creation of an effect." This is in direct contradiction to knowledge, although one of course can know how to create an effect.

Opposed to knowledge we have the neglected half of existence, which is the *creation* of knowledge, the creation of data, the creation of thought, the causative consideration, self-evolved ideas as opposed to ideas otherwise evolved. The reason Scientology is such a fascinating study is that it takes apart the other fellow's ideas and permits one to create some of his own. Scientology gives us the common denominators of objects, energies, spaces, universes, livingness and thought itself.

There is *cause* and *effect*. Cause could be defined as emanation. It could be defined also, for purposes of communication, as source-point. If you consider a river flowing to the sea, the place where it began would be the source-point or cause, and the place where it went into the sea would be the effect-point, and the sea would be the effect of the river. The man firing the gun is cause; the man receiving the bullet is effect. The one making a statement is causing a communication, the one receiving the statement is the effect of the communication. A basic definition of communication is cause-distance-effect.

Almost all anxieties and upsets in human relations come about through an imbalance of cause and effect.

One must be willing at once to cause new data, statements, assumptions, considerations, and to receive ideas, assumptions, considerations.

So great is the anxiety of a thetan to cause an effect that he closely approaches those things which can cause an effect upon him. Thus a thetan becomes trapped. On the face of it so few thetans make causative data and so many receive data that it would seem, in view of the fact that a thetan can be touched only by his own consideration, that thetans are more anxious for effects than to be cause;

however, this is not true in practice. In a game one seeks to cause an effect and to receive no-effect.

It is learned under close experiments that there is nothing a thetan actually disdains on an effect level. He pretends not to like or enjoy certain effects and protests against them, but he knows very well that the mechanism of protest causes the effect to approach more closely as a general rule. This came about by his repeated failure in games. Insisting on no-effect for himself, he lost. Then he had to say he liked the effect.

The prevailing anxiety then becomes to be an effect, not to be a cause. The entire subject of responsibility is a study of cause and effect in that a person who wants no responsibility is anxious to be an effect only, and a person who can assume responsibility must also be willing to be causative.

A thetan can be swung into a "state of consideration" by observing that it is commonly held by others. This keeps him in the universe and this keeps him being effect.

Study, investigation, receiving education and similar activity are all effect activities and result in the assumption of less responsibility. Thus, while it is true that a thetan cannot actually get into trouble, he can, by agreeing with the current agreed-upon thought in the universe where he finds himself, take a pattern of thinkingness which makes him less effective because he wishes to be an effect. If he feels he must gather all of his data from elsewhere, he is then the effect of knowledge, the effect of universes and postulates, and he tends to reduce his own ability to form or make knowledge.

In Scientology we can communicate in full these circumstances since we are only calling to attention the pattern which an individual himself already holds, thus we are not actually teaching him anything. We are only pointing out things he has already agreed with or himself caused.

It is only generally true that an individual is responsible for everything that happens to him. When an individual, wishing to cause many interesting effects, chooses to go into many universes or traps, he can become confused about what he is doing, where he is or what it is all about. Scientology points out that this can be seen or changed from a person's own viewpoint to bring about a change in his own condition.

As an example, a thetan has come to "believe" that the right way to get along in life is to do just as father did. This is an invitation to being in father's universe. Later on he changes his mind about this, but he finds himself still in father's universe and doesn't like it. He would be more effective, more capable, if he were not now in father's universe. Customarily, in these unenlightened times, he waits for death to separate himself from the environment in which he finds himself and puts up with it until then. It is not necessary to do this now that we have Scientology. He can at any moment, given the proper steerage, vacate any trap in which he finds himself and begin again on a new series of considerations.

We cannot then talk about knowledge as a totality. It is a

single datum. The thirst for knowledge would be the thirst for other thetans' postulates and would lead one to forget that he himself has been a party to the making of these postulates and that he himself had to follow a certain course in order to put himself in reach of other thetans' postulates.

(Note to Translators: Lacking a proper English word for "causative thinking", the word "postulate" has been used in slight difference to its English definition. If there is a word in your language which means "self-impulsion" or "creation of a thought", use that instead of "postulate".)

Because one is the effect of knowledge, causing data, considerations or "facts" to come into being separates one in distance from being an effect. If one is very anxious to be an effect and if this is his basic consideration, he will not take well to causing information to come into existence, but in order to get him out of the traps in which he finds himself, it is necessary to some degree that he do so.

Causing few barriers or traps, the individual then loses control over barriers or traps; wishing to be an effect, of course he must lose control of barriers and traps, otherwise he cannot be entrapped by them. The thing to do to free him from a trap is to have him find what parts of the trap he himself is willing to create, own, have or possess. This places the barriers (which can be spaces, energy movements or obstacles) under his control, and his postulating that he can have or possess this or that causes him to be willing to be or occupy the trap. The moment this occurs he is no longer in the trap, or even if he is still in it to some degree he does not object to it and can leave it when he wishes.

Civilization and Savagery

The way to paralyze a nation entirely and to make it completely ungovernable would be to forbid education of any kind within its borders and to inculcate into every person within it the feeling that he must not receive any information from anybody about anything. To make a nation governable it is necessary to hold a kindly view of education and to honor educative persons and measures. To conquer a land it is not necessarily efficient to overwhelm it with guns. Once this is done it is necessary to apply educative measures in order to bring about some sort of agreement amongst the people themselves, as well as between the conqueror and the subdued. Only in this way could one have a society, a civilization or, as we say in Scientology, a smoothly running game.

In other words, two extremes could be reached, neither one of which is desirable for the individual. The first extreme could be reached by emphasis only upon self-created data or information. This would bring about not only a lack of interpersonal relations, but also an anxiety to have an effect which would, as it does in barbaric peoples, result in social cruelty unimaginable in a civilized nation. The other extreme would be to forbid in its entirety any self-created information and to condone only data or considerations generated by others than self. Here we would create an individual with no responsibility, so easily handled that he would be only a puppet.

Self-created data is then not a bad thing, neither is education, but one without the other to hold it in some balance will bring about a no-game condition or a no-civilization. Just as individuals can be seen by observing nations, so we see the African tribesman, with his complete contempt for truth and his emphasis on brutality and savagery for others but not himself, is a no-civilization. And we see at the other extreme China, slavishly dedicated to ancient scholars, incapable of generating within herself sufficient rulers to continue, without bloodshed, a nation.

We have noted the individual who must be the only one who can make a postulate or command, whose authority is dearer to him than the comfort or state of millions who have suffered from such men (Napoleon, Hitler, Kaiser Wilhelm, Frederick of Prussia, Genghis Khan, Attila). We have known, too, the scholar who has studied himself into blindness and is the world's greatest authority on government or some such thing, who yet cannot himself manage his bank account or a dog with any certainty. Here we have, in either case, a total imbalance. The world shaker is himself unwilling to be any effect of any kind (and all the men named here were arrant personal cowards) and we have the opposite, a man who would not know what you were talking about if you told him to get an idea of his own.

We see another example of this in the fundamental laws of warfare. A body of troops, to be effective, must be able to attack and to defend. Its implements must be divided 50% for attack and 50% for defense. In other words, even in a crude activity such as warfare, we find that no successful outcome is possible unless the troops can devote half of their energies to attack and half of them to defense.

In the much broader view of life we discover on any dynamic that success or a game or activity or life itself depends upon being willing to be cause as well as willing to be an effect. He who would give must be willing to receive. He who would receive must be willing to give. When these tenets are violated, the most fundamental principle of human relationships is violated, and the result is a no-game condition such as aberration, insanity, anti-socialness, criminality, inactivity, laziness, tiredness, mania, fanaticism and all the other things against which men protest. But imbalances between cause and effect also enter randomities (unpredicted motions) into the game of life and cannot be neglected in their potential for creating a game.

Any information is valuable to the degree that you can use it. In other words, any information is valuable to the degree that you can make it yours. Scientology, of all the sciences, does not teach you—it only reminds you, for the information was yours in the first place. It is not only the science of life, but it is an account of what you were doing before you forgot what you were doing.

CHAPTER NINE

KNOW AND NOT-KNOW

It is a mechanism of thinkingness, whether one is postulating or receiving information, that one retain one's ability to know. It is equally important that one retain one's ability to not-know. Thought consists entirely of knowing and not-knowing and the shades of gray between.

You will discover that most people are trying not to remember. In other words, they are trying to not-know. Education can only become burdensome when one is unable to not-know it. It is necessary that one be able to create, to receive, to know, and to not-know information, data and thoughts. Lacking any one of these skills, for they are skills, no matter how native they are to the individual, one is apt to get into a chaos of thinkingness or creatingness or livingness.

You can look at any eccentric or aberrated person and discover rapidly, by an inspection of him, which one of these four factors he is violating. He either is unable to know or not-know his own created thoughts, or he is unable to know or not-know the thoughts of others. Somewhere, for some reason best known to him, in his anxiety to be part of the game, he has shelved or lost one of these abilities.

Time is a process of knowing in the present and not-knowing in the future or the past. Remembering is the process of knowing the past; prediction is the process of knowing the future. Forgetting is the process of not-knowing the past, and living "only for today" is the process of not-knowing the future.

Exercises in these various items rehabilitate not only the sanity or ability of the individual, but his general capability in living and playing the game.

CHAPTER TEN

THE GOAL OF SCIENTOLOGY

The end object of Scientology is not the making into nothing of all of existence or the freeing of the individual of any and all traps everywhere. The goal of Scientology is the making of the individual capable of living a better life in his own estimation and with his fellows, and the playing of a better game.

CHAPTER ELEVEN

SCIENTOLOGY PROCESSING

Scientology is applied in many ways to many fields. One particular and specialized method of application of Scientology is its use on individuals and groups of people in the eradication of physical problems deriving from mental states and the improvement of their abilities and intelligence. By processing is meant the verbal exercising of an individual (preclear) in exact Scientology processes. There is a great deal of terminology and precision in these processes and their use, and they are not combinable with older mental activities such as psychiatry, psychology, psychoanalysis, yoga, massage, etc. However, these processes are capable of addressing or treating the same ills of the mind as are delineated by older methodology, with the addition that Scientology is alone in its ability to successfully eradicate those psychosomatic problems to which it is addressed. It is the only science or study known which is capable of uniformly producing marked and significant increases in intelligence and general ability.

Scientology processing amongst other things can improve the intelligence quotient of an individual, his ability or desire to communicate, his social attitudes, his capability and domestic harmony, his fertility, his artistic creativity, his reaction time and his health.

An additional sphere of activity allied to processing is preventive Scientology. In this branch of processing, an individual is freed from assuming states lower than those he has already suffered from. In other words, the progress of tendencies, neuroses, habits and deteriorating activities can be halted by Scientology or their occurrence can be prevented. This is done by processing the individual on standard Scientology processes without particular attention to the aberration involved.

Scientology processing is called "auditing", by which the auditor (practitioner) "listens, computes and commands". The auditor and preclear (person receiving auditing) are together out-of-doors or in a quiet place where they will not be disturbed or where they are not being subjected to interrupting influences. The purpose of the auditor is to give the preclear certain and exact commands which the preclear can follow and perform. The purpose of the auditor is to increase the ability of the preclear. The Auditor's Code is the governing set of rules for the general activity of auditing. The Code follows:

The Auditor's Code

1. Do not evaluate for the preclear.
2. Do not invalidate or correct the preclear's data.
3. Use the processes which improve the preclear's case.
4. Keep all appointments once made.
5. Do not process a preclear after 10 p.m.
6. Do not process a preclear who is improperly fed or who has not received enough rest.
7. Do not permit a frequent change of auditors.
8. Do not sympathize with the preclear.
9. Never permit the preclear to end the session on his own independent decision.

10. Never walk off from a preclear during a session.
11. Never get angry with a preclear.
12. Always reduce every communication lag encountered by continued use of the same question or process.
13. Always continue a process as long as it produces change and no longer.
14. Be willing to grant beingness to the preclear.
15. Never mix the processes of Scientology with those of various other practices.
16. Maintain two-way communication with the preclear.
17. Never use Scientology to obtain personal and unusual favors or unusual compliance from the preclear for the auditor's own personal profit.
18. Estimate the current case of your preclear with reality and do not audit another imagined case.
19. Do not explain, justify, or make excuses for any auditor mistakes whether real or imagined.

The Auditor's Code governs the activity of the auditor during sessions. The activity of the Scientologist in general is governed by another broader code.

The Code of a Scientologist

As a Scientologist, I pledge myself to the code of Scientology for the good of all:

1. To hear or speak no word of disparagement to the press, public or preclears concerning any of my fellow Scientologists, our professional organization or those whose names are closely connected to this Science, nor to place in danger any such person.
2. To use the best I know of Scientology to the best of

my ability to better my preclears, groups and the world.

3. To refuse to accept for processing and to refuse to accept money from any preclear or group I feel I cannot honestly help.

4. To deter to the fullest extent of my power anyone misusing or degrading Scientology to harmful ends.

5. To prevent the use of Scientology in advertisements of other products.

6. To discourage the abuse of Scientology in the press.

7. To employ Scientology to the greatest good of the greatest number of dynamics.

8. To render good processing, sound training and good discipline to those students or peoples entrusted to my care.

9. To refuse to impart the personal secrets of my preclears.

10. To engage in no unseemly disputes with the uninformed on the subject of my profession.

11. To completely refrain from discussing the case of another auditor's preclear with that preclear, or within his hearing.

As it can be seen, both of these codes are designed to protect the preclear as well as Scientology and the auditor in general. As these codes evolve from many years of observation and experience by a great number of people, it can be said that they are intensely important and are probably complete. Failure to observe them has resulted in a failure of Scientology. Scientology can do what it can do only when it is used within the limits of these two codes. Thus it can be seen that the interjection of peculiarities or practices by the auditor into Scientology processing can actually nullify and eradicate the benefits of that processing. Any hope or promise in Scientology is conditional upon its good use by the individual and its use in particular within the limits of these two codes.

The Conditions of Auditing

Certain definite conditions must prevail and a certain methodology must be followed in order that processing may be beneficial to its fullest extent.

Probably the first condition is a good grasp of Scientology as a science and its mission in the world.

The second condition would be a relaxed state of mind on the part of the auditor and the confidence that his use of Scientology upon the preclear will not produce a harmful result.

The third requisite should be finding a preclear. By this it is literally meant that one should discover somebody willing to be processed, and, having discovered one so willing, should then make sure that he is aware that he is there being processed.

The fourth requisite would be a quiet place in which to audit, with every precaution taken that the preclear will not be interrupted or burst in upon or unduly startled during processing.

CHAPTER TWELVE

EXACT PROCESSES

Auditing
Game and No-Game Conditions

In Scientology, the most important single elements to the auditor are *Game Conditions* and *No-Game Conditions*. Reason—all games are aberrative.

All processing is directed toward game conditions. Little or no processing is directed toward no-game conditions. Therefore, it is of the utmost importance to know exactly what these are, for one could be superficial about it and lose.

Rule—all Games are aberrative, some are fun.

The Elements of Games to auditors are:

A game consists of freedoms, barriers and purposes.

In a game one's own team or self must receive no-effect and must deliver an effect upon the other team or opponent.

A game should have space and, preferably, a playing field.

A game is played in the same time continuum for both sides (all players).

A game must have something which one does not have in order for it to be won.

Some part of the dynamics must be excluded for a game condition to exist. The amount of the dynamics excluded represents the tone of the game.

Games occur only when there is intention opposing intention, purpose opposing purpose.

A scarcity of games forces the preclear to accept less desirable games.

Participation in any game (whether it be the game of sick-man, jealous-wife or polio) is preferable to being in a no-game condition.

The type of game entered by a person is determined by his consideration as to how much and what kind of an effect he may receive while trying to deliver an effect.

Games are the basic mechanism for continuing attention.

To play a game one must be able to not-know his past and future and not-know his opponent's complete intentions.

Game Conditions are:
    Attention
    Identity
    Effect on Opponents

No-effect on Self
Can't Have on opponents and goals and their areas
Have on tools of play, own goals and field
Purpose
Problems of play
Self-determinism
Opponents
The possibility of loss
The possibility of winning
Communication
Non-arrival

No-Game Conditions are:
Knowing All
Not-Knowing Everything
Serenity
Namelessness
No-effect on opponent
Effect on self or team
Have everything
Can't Have nothing
Solutions
Pan-Determinism
Friendship with All
Understanding
Total Communication
No Communication
Win
Lose
No Universe
No Playing Field
Arrival
Death

Process only with those conditions listed as Game Conditions. Do not process directly toward those conditions listed as No-Game Conditions. So doing, the auditor will run out (erase) the aberrative effect of games and restore an ability to play a game.

Identities—Valences

There are four identities or valences.

When one is in his "own" valence he is said to be "himself".

As he departs from his own identity he comes in to the following:

Exchanged Valence: One has directly superimposed the identity of another on his own. Example—Daughter becomes own mother to some degree. Remedy—One directly runs out mother.

Attention Valence: One has become the valence B because one wants attention from C. Example—One becomes mother because mother received attention from father while self did not. Remedy—Run out father even though preclear appears in valence of mother.

Synthetic Valence: One takes a valence about which he has been told. Example—Mother tells child false things about father, accuses child of being like father, with result that child is forced into father's valence. Remedy—Run out mother even though preclear does not seem to be near mother's valence.

Auditing Procedures

All requisites for auditing from here on are entirely concerned with procedures and processes. By auditing procedure is meant the general model of how one goes about addressing a preclear. This includes an ability to place one question worded exactly the same way over and over again to the preclear no matter how many times the preclear has answered the question. It should include the ability to acknowledge with a "good" and "all right" every time a preclear executes or completes the execution of a command. It should include the ability to accept a communication from the preclear. When the preclear has something to say, the auditor should acknowledge the fact that he has received the preclear's communication and should pay some attention to the communication.

Procedure also includes the ability to sense when the preclear is being over-strained by processing or is being unduly annoyed and to handle such crises in the session to prevent the preclear from leaving. An auditor should also have the ability of handling startling remarks or occurrences by the preclear. An auditor should also have the knack of preventing the preclear from talking obsessively since prolonged conversation markedly reduces the havingness of the preclear, and the sooner long dissertations by the preclear are cut off the better for the session in general.

Processes as distinct from procedures consist of utilizing the principle of the gradient scale to the end of placing the preclear in better control of himself, his mind, the people and the universe around him.

By gradient scale is meant a proceeding from simplicity toward greater difficulty, giving the preclear always no more than he can do, but giving him as much as he can do until he can handle a great deal. The idea here is to give the preclear nothing but wins and to refrain from giving the preclear losses in the game of processing. Thus it can be seen that processing is a team activity and is not itself a game whereby the auditor opposes and seeks to defeat the preclear and the preclear seeks to defeat the auditor, for when this condition exists little results in processing.

The earliest stage of auditing consists in taking over control of the preclear so as to restore to the preclear more control of himself than he has had. The most fundamental step is then location, whereby the preclear is made to be aware of the fact that he is in an auditing room, that an auditor is present and that the preclear is being a preclear.

Those conditions will become quite apparent if one realizes that it would be very difficult for a son to process a father. A father is not likely to recognize anything else than the boy he raised in his auditor. Therefore the father would have to be made aware of the fact that the son was a competent practitioner before the father could be placed under control in processing. One of the most elementary commands in Scientology is "Look at me, who am I?" After a preclear has been asked to do this many times until he can do so quickly and accurately and without protest, it can be said that the preclear will have "found" the auditor.

The preclear is asked by the auditor to control, which is to say, start, change and stop (the anatomy of control) anything he is capable of controlling. In a very bad case this might be a very small object being pushed around on a table, being started and changed and stopped each time specifically and only at the auditor's command until the preclear himself realizes that he himself can start, change and stop the object. Sometimes four or five hours spent in this exercise are very well spent on a very difficult preclear.

The preclear is then asked to start, change and stop his own body under the auditor's specific and precise direction. In all of his commands the auditor must be careful never to give a second command before the first one has been fully obeyed. A preclear in this procedure is walked around the room and is made to start, change the direction of and stop his body, emphasizing one of these at a time, until he realizes that he can do so with ease. Only now could it be said that a session is well in progress or that a preclear is securely under the auditor's command.

It should be noted especially that the goal of Scientology is better self-determinism for the preclear. This rules out at once hypnotism, drugs, alcohol or other control mechanisms used by other and older therapies. It will be found that such things are not only not necessary, but they are in direct opposition to the goals of greater ability for the preclear.

The principal points of concentration for the auditor now become the ability of the preclear to have, the ability of the preclear to not-know, and the ability of the preclear to play a game.

An additional factor is the ability of the preclear to be himself and not a number of other people, such as his father, his mother, his marital partner or his children.

The ability of the preclear is increased by addressing to him the process known as the Trio. These are three questions, or rather commands.

1. "Look around here and tell me what you could have."
2. "Look around here and tell me what you would permit to remain in place."
3. "Look around here and tell me with what you could dispense."

No. 1 above is used usually about ten times, then No. 2 is used five times, and No. 3 is used once. This ratio of ten, five and one would be an ordinary or routine approach to havingness. The end in view is to bring the preclear into a condition whereby he can possess or own or have whatever he sees, without further conditions, ramifications or restrictions. This is the most therapeutic of all processes, elementary as it might seem. It is done without too much two-way communication or discussion with the preclear, and it is done until the preclear can answer questions one, two and three equally well. It should be noted at once that twenty-five hours of use of this process by an auditor upon a preclear brings about a very high rise in tone. By saying twenty-five hours it is intended to give the idea of the length of time the process should be used. As it is a strain on the usual person to repeat the same question over and over, it will be seen that an auditor should be well disciplined or very well trained before he audits.

In the case of a preclear who is very unable, "Can't have" is substituted for "have", etc., in each of the above questions for a few hours, until the preclear is ready for the Trio in its "have" form. This can-can't is the plus and minus aspect of all thought and in Scientology is called by a specialized word *dichotomy*.

The rehabilitation of the ability of the preclear to not-know is also rehabilitation of the preclear in the time stream since the process of time consists of knowing the moment and not-knowing the past and not-knowing the future simultaneously. This process, like all other Scientology processes, is repetitive. The process is run, ordinarily, only after the preclear is in very good condition and is generally run in an exterior well inhabited place. Here the auditor, without exciting public comment, indicates a person and asks the preclear "Can you not-know something about that person?" The auditor does not permit the preclear to "not-know" things which the preclear already doesn't know. The preclear "not-knows" only those things which are visible and apparent about the person. This is also run on objects in the environment such as walls, floors, chairs and other things. The auditor should not be startled when for the preclear large chunks of the environment start to disappear. This is ordinary routine and in effect the preclear should make the entirety of the environment disappear at his own command. The environment does not disappear for the auditor. The end goal of this "not-know" process is the disappearance of the entire universe, under the preclear's control, but only for the preclear.

It will be discovered while running this that the preclear's "havingness" may deteriorate. If this happens, he was not run enough on the Trio before he was run on this process. It is only necessary in such a case to intersperse

"Look around here and tell me what you could have" with the "not-know" command to keep the preclear in good condition. Drop of havingness is manifested by nervous agitation, obsessive talk or semi-unconsciousness or "dopiness" on the part of the preclear. These manifestations indicate only reduction of havingness.

The reverse of the question here is "Tell me something that you would be willing to have that person (indicated by the auditor) not-know about you." Both sides of the question have to be run (audited). This process can be continued for twenty-five hours or even fifty or seventy-five hours of auditing with considerable benefit so long as it does not react too violently upon the preclear in terms of loss of havingness.

It should be noted that, in running either havingness or "not-know" on a preclear, the preclear may "exteriorize". In other words, it may become apparent, either by his observation or because the preclear informs him, that the auditor has "exteriorized" a preclear. Under "The Parts of Man" section there is an explanation of this phenomenon. In modern auditing the auditor does not do anything odd about this beyond receive and be interested in the preclear's statement of the fact. The preclear should not be permitted to become alarmed since it is a usual manifestation. A preclear is in better condition and will audit better exteriorized than "in his head".

Understanding that an actual ability to "not-know" is an ability to erase the past by self-command without suppressing it with energy or going into any other method is necessary to help the preclear. It is the primary rehabilitation in terms of knowingness. Forgetting is a lower manifestation than "not-knowingness".

The third ability to be addressed by the auditor is the ability of the preclear to play a game. First and foremost in the requisites to playing a game is the ability to control. One must be able to control something in order to participate in a game. Therefore the general rehabilitation of control by starting, changing and stopping things is a rehabilitation in the ability to play a game. When a preclear refuses to recover, it is because the preclear is using his state as a game, and does not believe that there is any better game for him to play than the state he is in. He may protest if this is called a game. Nevertheless, any condition will surrender if the auditor has the preclear invent similar conditions or even tell lies about the existing condition. Inventing games or inventing conditions or inventing problems alike rehabil-itate the ability to play a game. Chief amongst these various rehabilitation factors are control (start, change and stop), problems, and the willingness to overwhelm or be over-whelmed. One ceases to be able to have games when one loses control over various things, when one becomes short of problems and when one is unwilling to be overwhelmed (in other words, to lose) or to overwhelm (to win). It will be found while running havingness as in the Trio above that one may run down the ability to play a game, since havingness is the reward of a game in part.

In the matter of problems it will be seen that these are completely necessary to the playing of a game. The anatomy of a problem is intention versus intention. This is, of course, in essence the purpose of all games, to have two sides, each one with an opposed intention. Technically a problem is two or more purposes in conflict. It is very simple to detect whether or not the preclear is suffering from a scarcity of games. The preclear who needs more games clutches to himself various present-time problems. If an auditor is confronted with a preclear who is being obsessed by a problem in present time he knows two things: (1) that the preclear's ability to play a game is low, and (2) that he must run an exact process at once to rehabilitate the preclear in session.

It often happens at the beginning of an auditing session that the preclear has encountered a heavy present-time problem between sessions. The preclear must always be consulted before the session is actually in progress as to whether or not he has "anything worrying" him. To a preclear who is worried about some present-time situation or problem no other process has any greater effectiveness than the following one. The auditor after a very *brief* discussion of the problem asks the preclear "to invent" a problem of comparable magnitude. He may have to re-word this request to make the preclear understand it completely, but the auditor wants in essence the preclear to invent or create a problem he considers similar to the problem he has. If the preclear is unable to do this, it is necessary then to have him lie about the problem which he has. Lying is the lowest order of creativeness. After he has lied about the problem for a short time, it will be found that he will be able to invent problems. He should be made to invent problem after problem until he is no longer concerned with his present-time problem.

The auditor should understand that a preclear who is "now willing to do something about the problem" has not been run long enough on the invention of problems of comparable magnitude. As long as the preclear is attempting to *do* something about the problem, the problem is still of obsessive importance to him. No session can be continued successfully until such a present-time problem is entirely flat, and it has been the experience, when a present-time problem was not completely eradicated by this process, that the remainder of the session or indeed the entire course of auditing may be interrupted.

When a preclear does not seem to be advancing under auditing, a thing which he does markedly and observedly, it must then be supposed that the preclear has a present-time problem which has not been eradicated and which must be handled in auditing. Although the auditor gives the preclear to understand that he too believes this present-time problem is extremely important, the auditor should not believe that this process will not handle *any* present-time problem, since it will. This process should be done on some preclears in company with the Trio.

If the preclear is asked to "lie about" or "invent a problem of comparable magnitude," and while doing so becomes agitated or unconscious or begins to talk wildly or obsessively, it must be assumed that he will have to have some havingness run on him until the agitation or manifestation ceases so that the problem of comparable magnitude process can be resumed.

Another aspect of the ability to play a game is the willingness to win and the willingness to lose. An individual has to be willing to be cause or willing to be an effect. As far as games are concerned, this is reduced to a willingness to win and a willingness to lose. People become afraid of defeat and afraid of failure. The entire anatomy of failure is only that one's postulates or intentions are reversed in action. For instance, one intends to strike a wall and strikes it. That is a win. One intends not to strike a wall and doesn't strike it. That is again a win. One intends not to strike a wall and strikes it. That is a lose. One intends to strike a wall and can't strike it. This is again a lose. It will be seen in this as well as other things that the most significant therapy there is is changing one's mind. All things are as one considers they are and no other way. If it is sufficiently simple to give the definition of winning and losing, so it is simple to process the matter.

This condition is best expressed, it appears, in processing by a process known as "overwhelming". An elementary way of running this is to take the preclear outside where there are numbers of people to observe and, indicating a person, to ask the preclear "What could overwhelm that person?" When the preclear answers this, he is asked about the same person, "What could that person overwhelm?" He is then asked as the third question, "Look around here and tell me what you could have?" These three questions are run one after the other. Then another person is chosen and then the three questions are asked again.

This process can be varied in its wording, but the central idea must remain as above. The preclear can be asked, "What would you permit to overwhelm that person?" and "What would you permit that person to overwhelm?" and of course "Look around here and tell me what you could have?" This is only one of a number of possible processes on the subject of overwhelming, but it should be noted that asking the preclear to think of things which would overwhelm *him* could be fatal to the case. Where over-whelming is handled, the preclear should be given a detached view.

A counter-position to havingness processes, but one which is less therapeutic, is "separateness". One asks the preclear to look around and discover things which are separate from things. This is repeated over and over. It is, however, destructive of havingness even though it will occasionally prove beneficial.

It will be seen that havingness (barriers), "not-knowingness" (being in present time and not in the past or the future), purposes (problems, antagonists, or intention-counter-intention), and separateness (freedom) will cover the anatomy of games. It is not to be thought, however, that havingness addresses itself only to games. Many other factors enter into it. In amongst all of these, it is of the greatest single importance.

One addresses in these days of Scientology the subjective self, the mind, as little as possible. One keeps the preclear alert to the broad environment around him. An address to the various energy patterns of the mind is less beneficial than exercises which directly approach other people or the physical universe. Therefore, asking a preclear to sit still and answer the question "What could you have?", when it is answered by the preclear from his experience or on the score of things which are not present, is found to be non-therapeutic and is found instead to decrease the ability and intelligence of the preclear. This is what is known as a subjective (inside the mind only) process.

These are the principal processes which produce marked gains. There are other processes and there are combinations of processes, but these given here are the most important. A Scientologist knowing the mind completely can of course do many "tricks" with the conditions of people to improve them. One of these is the ability to address a psychosomatic illness such as a crippled leg which, having nothing physically wrong with it, yet is not usable. The auditor could ask the preclear "Tell me a lie about your leg" with a possible relief of the pain or symptoms. Asking the preclear repeatedly "Look around here and tell me something your leg could have" would undoubtedly release the somatic. Asking the preclear with the bad leg "What problem could your leg be to you?" or desiring him to "Invent a problem of comparable magnitude to your leg" would produce a distinct change in the condition of the leg. This would apply to any other body part or organ. It would also apply, strangely enough, to the preclear's possessions. If a preclear had a vehicle or cart which was out of repair or troublesome to him, one could ask him "What problem could a cart be to you?" and thus requesting him to invent many such problems one would discover that he had solved his problems with the cart. There is a phenomenon in existence that the preclear already has many set games, and when the auditor asks him to give some problems, he already has the manifestations of as-ising or erasing taking place. Thought erases; therefore the number of problems or games the preclear could have would be reduced by asking him to recount those which he already has. Asking the preclear to describe his symptoms is far less therapeutic and may result in a worsening of those symptoms, contrary to what some schools of thought have believed in the past but which accounts for their failures.

There are specific things which one must avoid in auditing. These follow:

1. *Significances*. The easiest thing a thetan does is change his mind. The most difficult thing he does is handle the environment in which he finds himself situated. Therefore, asking a thetan to run out various ideas is a fallacy. It is a mistake. Asking the preclear to think over something can also be an error. Asking a preclear to do exercises which concern his mind alone can be entirely fatal. A preclear is processed between himself and his environment. If he is processed between himself and his mind, he is processed up too short a view and his condition will worsen.

2. *Two-way communication*. There can be far too much two-way communication or far too much communication in an auditing session. Communication involves the reduction of havingness. Letting a preclear talk on and on or obsessively is to let a preclear reduce his havingness. The preclear who is permitted to go on talking will talk himself down the tone scale and into a bad condition. It is better for the auditor simply and discourteously to tell a preclear to "shut up" than to have the preclear run himself "out of the bottom" on havingness. You can observe this for yourself if you permit a person who is not too able to talk about his troubles to keep on talking. He will begin to talk more and more hectically. He is reducing his havingness. He will eventually talk himself down the tone scale into apathy at which time he will be willing to tell you (as you insist upon it) that he "feels better" when, as a matter of fact, he is actually worse. Asking a preclear "How do you feel now?" can reduce his havingness since he looks over his

present-time condition and as-ises some mass.

3. *Too many processes*. It is possible to run a preclear on too many processes in too short a time with a reduction of the preclear's recovery. This is handled by observing the communication lag of the preclear. It will be discovered that the preclear will space his answers to a repeated question differently with each answer. When a long period ensues between the question and his answer to the question a second time, he is said to have a "communication lag". The "communication lag" is the length of time between the placing of the question by the auditor and the answering of that exact question by the preclear. It is not the length of time between the placing of the question by the auditor and some statement by the preclear.

It will be found that the communication lag lengthens and shortens on a repeated question. The question on the tenth time it has been asked may detect no significant lag. This is the time to stop asking that question since it now has no appreciable communication lag. One can leave any process when the communication lag for three successive questions is the same.

In order to get from one process to another, one employs a communication bridge which to a marked degree reduces the liability of too many processes. A communication bridge is always used.

Before a question is asked, the preclear should have the question discussed with him and the wording of the question agreed upon, as though he were making a contract with the auditor. The auditor says that he is going to have the preclear do certain things and finds out if it's all right with the preclear if the auditor asks him to do these things. This is the first part of a communication bridge. It precedes all questions, but when one is changing from one process to another the bridge becomes a bridge indeed. One levels out the old process by asking the preclear whether or not he doesn't think it is safe to leave that process now. One discusses with the preclear the possible benefit received from the process and then tells the preclear that he is no longer going to use that process. Now he tells the preclear he is going to use a new process, describes the process and gets an agreement on it. When the agreement is achieved, then he uses this process. The communication bridge is used at all times. The last half of it, the agreement on a new process, is used always before any process is begun.

4. *Failure to handle the present-time problem.* Probably more cases are stalled or found unable to benefit in processing because of the neglect of the present-time problem, as covered above, than any other single item.

5. *Unconsciousness, "dopiness" or agitation on the part of the preclear* is not a mark of good condition. It is a loss of havingness. The preclear must never be processed into unconsciousness or "dopiness". He should always be kept alert. The basic phenomenon of unconsciousness is "a flow which has flowed too long in one direction." If one talks too long at somebody he will render him unconscious. In order to wake up the target of all that talk, it is necessary to get the person to do some talking. It is simply necessary to reverse any flow to make unconsciousness disappear, but this is normally cared for in modern Scientology by running the Trio above.

The Future of Scientology

   With man now equipped with weapons sufficient to destroy all mankind on Earth, the emergence of a new science capable of handling man is vital. Scientology is such a science. It was born in the same crucible as the atomic bomb. The basic intelligence of Scientology came from nuclear physics, higher mathematics and the understanding of the ancients in the East. Scientology can and does do exactly what it says it can do. In Washington, D.C., there is an enormous file cabinet filled with thousands of case histories, fully validated and sworn to, which attest the scientific thoroughness of Scientology. With Scientology man can prevent insanity, criminality and war. It is for man to use. It is for the betterment of man. The primary race of Earth is not between one nation and another today. The only race that matters at this moment is the one being run between Scientology and the atomic bomb. The history of man, as has been said by well-known authorities, may well depend upon which one wins.

THE AIMS OF SCIENTOLOGY

A civilization without insanity, without criminals and without war, where the able can prosper and honest beings can have rights, and where Man is free to rise to greater heights, are the aims of Scientology.

First announced to an enturbulated world fifteen years ago, these aims are well within the grasp of our technology.

Non-political in nature, Scientology welcomes any individual of any creed, race or nation.

We seek no revolution. We seek only evolution to higher states of being for the individual and for Society.

We are achieving our aims.

After endless millenia of ignorance about himself, his mind and the Universe, a breakthrough has been made.

Other efforts Man has made have been surpassed.

The combined truths of Fifty Thousand years of thinking men, distilled and amplified by new discoveries about Man, have made for this success.

We welcome you to Scientology. We only expect of you your help in achieving our aims and helping others. We expect you to be helped.

Scientology is the most vital movement on Earth today.

In a turbulent world the job is not easy. But then, if it were, we wouldn't have to be doing it.

We respect Man and believe he is worthy of help. We respect you and believe you too can help.

Scientology does not owe its help. We have done nothing to cause us to propitiate. Had we done so we would not now be bright enough to do what we are doing.

Man suspects all offers of help. He has often been betrayed, his confidence shattered. Too frequently he has given his trust and been betrayed. We may err, for we build a world with broken straws. But we will never betray your faith in us so long as you are one of us.

The sun never sets on Scientology.

And may a new day dawn for you, for those you love and for Man.

Our aims are simple if great.

And we will succeed, and are succeeding at each new revolution of the Earth.

Your help is acceptable to us.

Our help is yours.

L. RON HUBBARD
1965

L. RON HUBBARD

Scientology was developed by L. Ron Hubbard, an American writer and philosopher.

It was completed after 35 years of research.

Hubbard was born in Tilden, Nebraska, March 13, 1911.

Much of Hubbard's early youth was spent in the American West and he travelled extensively in Asia as a young man.

He studied Science and Mathematics in the Department of Engineering at George Washington University, and later attended Princeton University. In 1950 he was awarded an honorary degree from Sequoia University.

Before World War II he was well known in explorational circles and is to this day a member of the Explorers Club.

He wrote and published over 15,000,000 words of articles and novels of all kinds before World War II.

Crippled and blind at the end of the war, he resumed his studies of philosophy and by his discoveries recovered so fully that he was re-classified in 1949 for full combat duty. It is a matter of medical record that he has twice been pronounced dead and that in 1950 he was given a perfect score on mental and physical fitness reports.

Revolted by war and Man's inhumanity to Man, he resigned his commission rather than assist government research projects.

He published his original thesis on his work and the startling popularity of the thesis brought publishers to offer him a contract for a popular work on the subject which in 1950 soared to the top of the best-seller lists and stayed there.

Hubbard has a lovely wife, Mary Sue Hubbard, and four charming children.

Unlike any other philosopher in any age, Hubbard has led a very full and adventurous life. He has been the hero in numerous novels and even of a famous motion picture.

Probably no philosopher of modern times has had the popularity and appeal of Hubbard or such startling successes within his own lifetime.

ORDER YOUR BOOKS FROM
THESE CHURCHES
OF SCIENTOLOGY

UNITED STATES

WASHINGTON, D.C.
The Founding Church of Scientology
2125 "S" Street N.W.
Washington, D.C. 20008

LOS ANGELES
Church of Scientology of California
New American Saint Hill
2723 West Temple Street
Los Angeles, Calif. 90026

Church of Scientology of California
The New Los Angeles Organization
2005 West 9th Street
Los Angeles, California 90006

Church of Scientology
Advanced Organization
916 South Westlake
Los Angeles, Calif. 90006

Church of Scientology
Celebrity Centre
1551 North La Brea Ave.
Hollywood, Calif. 90028

SAN FRANCISCO
Church of Scientology of California
414 Mason Street
San Francisco, Calif. 94102

SACRAMENTO
Church of Scientology of California
819 19th Street
Sacramento, California 95814

BOSTON
Church of Scientology
of Boston
448 Beacon Street
Boston, Mass. 02115

ST. LOUIS
Church of Scientology of Missouri
3730 Lindell Blvd.
St. Louis, Missouri 63108

DETROIT
Church of Scientology of Michigan
19 Clifford
Detroit, Mich 48226

AUSTIN
Church of Scientology of Texas
2804 Rio Grande
Austin, Texas 78705

SEATTLE
Church of Scientology of Washington
1531 4th Avenue
Seattle, Wash. 98101

LAS VEGAS
Church of Scientology of Nevada
2108 Industrial Road
Las Vegas, Nev. 89102

MIAMI
Church of Scientology of Florida
1235 Brickell Avenue
Miami, Florida 33131

MINNEAPOLIS
Church of Scientology
of Minnesota
730 Hennepin Avenue
Minneapolis, Minn. 55403

NEW YORK
Church of Scientology of New York
30 West 74th Street
New York, New York 10023

BUFFALO
The Church of Scientology
New Buffalo Organization
1116 Elmwood Avenue
Buffalo, New York 14222

HAWAII
Church of Scientology of Hawaii
143 Nenue Street
Honolulu, Hawaii 96821

SAN DIEGO
Church of Scientology of San Diego
926 "C" Street
San Diego, Calif. 92101

PORTLAND
Church of Scientology of Portland
333 South West Park
Portland, Ore. 97205

PHILADELPHIA
The Church of Scientology of Philadelphia
8 West Lancaster Ave.
Ardmore, Penn 19003

CHICAGO
The Church of Scientology of Chicago
1555 Maple
Evanston, Ill. 60201

CANADA

TORONTO
Church of Scientology of Toronto
124 Avenue Road
Toronto, Ontario, Canada
M5R 2H5

OTTAWA
Church of Scientology
292 Somerset W.
Ottawa, Ontario, Canada
K2P 9Z9

MONTREAL
Church of Scientology
15 Notre Dame Ouest
Montreal, Quebec, Canada
H2Y 1B5

VANCOUVER
Church of Scientology of British Columbia
4857 Main Street
Vancouver, British Columbia
Canada V5V 3R8

ENGLAND

Hubbard College of Scientology
Saint Hill Manor
East Grinstead
Sussex, England RH19 4JY

Church of Scientology of Manchester
48 Faulkner Street
Manchester M1 4FH

LONDON
The Hubbard Scientology Organization
68 Tottenham Court Road
London W1, England

PLYMOUTH
Scientology Plymouth
39 Portland Square
Sherwell, Plymouth, Devon

SCOTLAND

EDINBURGH
H.A.P.I. Scotland Fleet House
20 Southbridge
Edinburgh 1, Scotland

DENMARK

COPENHAGEN
Church of Scientology of Denmark
Hovedvagtsgade 6
1103 Copenhagen K

Church of Scientology of Copenhagen
Fredericksborgvej 5
2400 Copenhagen NV
Denmark

Church of Scientology
Advanced Organization
and Saint Hill
Jernbanegade 6
1608 Copenhagen V
Denmark

SWEDEN

Church of Scientology of Sweden
Magasinsgatan 12
S-411 18 Goteborg, Sweden

MALMO
Church of Scientology of Malmo
Skomakaregatan 12
S-211 34 Malmo, Sweden

STOCKHOLM
Scientology Kyrkan
Kanmakaregatan 46
S-111 60 Stockholm, Sweden

HOLLAND
Scientology Kerk Nederland
261 Singel
Amsterdam C, Holland

GERMANY
Scientology Munchen
8000 Munchen 2
Lindwurmstrasse 29
Munich, Germany

FRANCE
Church of Scientology of Paris
12 rue de La Montagne Ste.
Genevieve, 75005 Paris, France

SOUTH AFRICA

JOHANNESBURG
Church of Scientology
of South Africa (Pty.) Ltd.
99 Polly St. Johannesburg,

PORT ELIZABETH
Church of Scientology
2 St. Christopher's
27 Westbourne Rd.
Port Elizabeth, S. Africa 6001

CAPETOWN
Church of Scientology of
South Africa (Pty.) Ltd.
Garmor House 127 Plein Street
Capetown, South Africa

DURBAN
Church of Scientology in
South Africa (Pty.) Ltd.
College House 57 College Lane
Durban, South Africa

PRETORIA
224 Central House
Cnr. Central & Pretorius Streets
Pretoria, South Africa

AUSTRALIA

ADELAIDE
Church of Scientology 57 Pulteney St.
Adelaide 5000,
So. Australia

MELBOURNE
Church of Scientology
724 Inkerman Road
North Caulfield 3161
Victoria, Australia

SYDNEY
Church of Scientology
1 Lee Street
Sydney 2000, New South Wales

PERTH
Church of Scientology
Pastoral House
156 St. George's Terrace.
Perth 5000,
W. Australia

NEW ZEALAND

AUCKLAND
Church of Scientology
of Auckland
Suites 1-4, 2nd Floor
Imperial Building
44 Queen Street
Auckland 1, New Zealand

RHODESIA

BULAWAYO
508 Kirrie Bldgs.
Abercorn Street
Bulawayo, Rhodesia

DATE DUE